MORAL LEADERSHIP
AND THE
AMERICAN PRESIDENCY

MORAL LEADERSHIP
AND THE
AMERICAN PRESIDENCY

Robert E. Denton, Jr.

JK
516
.D46
2005
west

ROWMAN & LITTLEFIELD PUBLISHERS, INC.
Lanham • Boulder • New York • Toronto • Oxford

ROWMAN & LITTLEFIELD PUBLISHERS, INC.

Published in the United States of America
by Rowman & Littlefield Publishers, Inc.
A wholly owned subsidiary of The Rowman & Littlefield Publishing Group, Inc.
4501 Forbes Boulevard, Suite 200, Lanham, Maryland 20706
www.rowmanlittlefield.com

P.O. Box 317, Oxford OX2 9RU, UK

Copyright © 2005 by Rowman & Littlefield Publishers, Inc.

All rights reserved. No part of this publication may be reproduced, stored in a retrieval system,
or transmitted in any form or by any means, electronic, mechanical, photocopying, recording,
or otherwise, without the prior permission of the publisher.

British Library Cataloguing in Publication Information Available

Library of Congress Cataloging-in-Publication Data

Denton, Robert E., Jr.
  Moral leadership and the American presidency / Robert E. Denton, Jr.
      p. cm.
  Includes bibliographical references and index.
  ISBN 0-7425-3948-2 (cloth : alk. paper)
  1. Presidents—United States—Psychology. 2. Presidents—United States—Conduct of life—
History. 3. Character—Political aspects—United States—History. 4. Presidents—United
States—Professional ethics. 5. Political leadership—United States. 6 United States—Politics
and government—Moral and ethical aspects. I. Title.
  JK516.D46 2005
  973'.099—dc22

                                                                        2005010744

Printed in the United States of America

∞™ The paper used in this publication meets the minimum requirements of American
National Standard for Information Sciences—Permanence of Paper for Printed Library
Materials, ANSI/NISO Z39.48-1992.

This book is dedicated to Walter Medlin, my grandfather, and Aubrey Hancock, my uncle, both long passed. When I was a child, Grandpa Medlin would talk about history, although for him, the events were life experiences. Uncle Aubrey, a history teacher, would share, for hours, stories of American presidents. I loved the stories, discussions, and times of sharing. Grandpa Medlin and Uncle Aubrey encouraged my questions, curiosity, and study. They provided me with a sense of confidence as well. Together, they are largely responsible for my love of history, my interest in the American presidency, and my personal love of teaching. As they undoubtedly knew, they made a difference in my life. With all my love, appreciation, and utmost admiration.

Contents

Preface

I have always been a fan of the American presidency as an institution and its occupants. At a very early age I loved books on American history and presidential memoirs. Throughout my academic career, both as a student and later as a teacher, my focus has been on politics, campaigns, and the presidency. I also have strong appreciation and admiration for leadership. I have had the privilege to serve in a wide variety of leadership positions ranging from student government to the military, to the corporate world, to academic departments and centers. I have also served under and with great leaders. Over the years I have become very interested in the subject of leadership: the qualities, traits, and even training of leaders.

I currently serve as director of the Major General W. Thomas Rice Center for Leader Development at Virginia Tech. One of my principal constituencies is the Corps of Cadets. These young men and women simply inspire me. They are dedicated, disciplined, and courageous. They are men and women of principle and character. More than 85 percent serve in the armed forces upon graduation. And yes, as of this date, they have lost four fellow brothers to the current war on terrorism. They follow numerous others from the Corps who made the ultimate sacrifice for this nation since 1872.

What I do know is that there is a vast difference between leadership and management. Leadership is more than a set of skills, traits, or knowledge. It is also about standards of conduct and modes of behavior. It is about values. It is difficult, at best. There is absolutely nothing "common" about being a genuine leader, but there is no higher calling or human service.

We have a crisis of leadership in America today. We are not electing the very best to public office nor are the best willing to serve. This is true from the most local of all elections to the pinnacle of power, the U.S. presidency. As a nation, we have lowered our standards and expectations of those who run and their performance in office, culminating with Bill Clinton. What is most alarming to me is that Americans generally accepted outrageous behavior without shame or outrage, mistakenly believing that the behaviors of public lying had no impact upon job performance. Private life does not impact public life.

At least in the aftermath of the presidential election of 2004, "moral values" was reported in exit polls as the primary issue of voter influence. Just prior to the election, some 71 percent of Americans, according to a Gallup poll, rated the state of "moral values" in America as "only fair" or "poor."[1] Yet many Americans ridicule and scorn George W. Bush's public professions of faith, claiming that religion makes him too arrogant, too closed minded, too judgmental, and too simplistic in worldviews.

This book is about moral presidential leadership and a call for the return of what some presidential scholars would describe as the "heroic" presidency. I attempt to make the argument that personal character and integrity of our presidents are essential and critical in today's world, even more so in a democracy. I also address the myth of separating private from public behaviors and how virtually everything presidents do or say influences their decisions and impacts the citizens in both obvious and subtle ways. Finally, I argue that if we want "better" leaders in the future, then we need to be "better" citizens.

In discussing this project with friends and colleagues, everyone, nearly to a person, warned me not to use the words "character," "integrity," or "moral." Such words as concepts are "too loaded," "too religious sounding," "too judgmental," especially for an academic! I was really taken aback by such comments. There was a time when institutions of higher learning were places of moral foundations and clear understandings of right and wrong, good and bad, where qualities of character and integrity were taught and reinforced. Unfortunately, that's certainly less the case today. Campuses, even more so than general society, are active havens of social and moral relativism. The prominent ideology of liberalism, in the worst sense, dominates.

First, as to my motives, I am not writing this book for my academic colleagues. I am sharing observations and making an argument for the importance of electing presidents who reflect the skills, qualities, and behaviors that epitomize authentic leadership. Second, for what it is worth, I am at the age now that I am not going to be intimidated to hold unorthodox or unpopular views. Nor am I going to be silent, especially on topics of great concern to me. Finally, the premise of this book is not an excuse to bash Bill Clinton or to praise George W. Bush. Yes, as a public leader and president, Clinton was very problematic with both obvious and yet-to-discover consequences for our nation. And yes, from a personal leadership perspective, Bush does provide a clear counter to Clinton. However, they both provide glimpses and examples of just part of my argument on moral leadership and the American presidency.

I wish to thank my colleagues in the Department of Communication at Virginia Tech. A faculty committed to scholarship productivity provides encouragement, even for an "older" colleague with administrative responsibilities. I also want to thank Jerry Niles, Dean of the College of Liberal Arts and Human Sciences; Richard Sorensen, Dean of the Pamplin College of Business; and Major General (retired) Jerrold Allen, Commandant of the Corps of Cadets, for their continued support of administrative, professional, and scholarly activities. As individuals, they are not only outstanding leaders, but they are indeed moral leaders reflecting the values of integrity, honesty, and trustworthiness. Unfortunately, based upon my life in academe, such leaders are not the norm. I genuinely admire and respect each of them. They have understood the importance of the right "mix" of teaching, writing, and outreach that makes my job a privilege and pleasure. They have supported me professionally, financially, and personally. I am very fortunate to work for such outstanding administrators who continue to serve as role models in every way.

Finally, I wish to thank members of my family who tolerate the long hours in the endeavors of teaching, research, and outreach. They sustain me, encourage me, and provide a sense of belonging and security that frees me to read, write, and pursue projects of interest. My boys, Bobby and Chris, are leaving the nest. They have become adults. I wish for them the benefit of good leaders, ethical public servants, and great presidents. My wife, Rachel, deserves special praise as a leader in her own right, my partner, my love, and my friend. Rachel, Bobby, and Chris, and yes, our little dog Daisy, provide the joys of my life well beyond academe. I come to cherish them even more with each passing day.

Note

1. "Bush Voters Support Active Government Role in Values Arena," Gallup Poll News Service, November 29, 2004, http://www.gallup.com/poll/content/print.aspx?ci=14158 (December 3, 2004).

1

Presidential Character: Does It Really Matter?

When in doubt, tell the truth. It will confound your enemies and astound your friends.

—MARK TWAIN

This is not a book about presidents per se. It is a book about the institutional presidency. And coming from academe, I must say from the outset that this is not so much an academic book or treatise as it is simply an argument about the importance of the symbolic and cultural role of the American presidency. Even more so, it is also a call, contrary to contemporary presidential scholarship, for the return of what some call the "heroic presidency." I believe leaders matter and they are not only important, but also essential to society. Presidents do more than initiate policy. They inspire and motivate a nation. The president is and should be a role model. The office reflects the collective values, hopes, and aspirations of the nation.

In 1992, Clinton promised a new era in American politics. He promised a "new covenant" between government and the public. Clinton also promised "the most ethical administration in history." Yet, as James Bovard observed, "after nearly eight years of his rule, America [was] bedeviled by independent counsels crowding Washington streets, cynicism as far as the eye can see, and more hostility to government agencies across the board."[1] He concludes, "the Clinton administration changed the political fabric of this nation and the political expectations of the

1

American people and the American media. Clinton's policies and rhetoric helped infantilize the American populace. The entire political system was subtly transformed year by year, crisis by crisis, hoax by hoax."[2]

In 2000, despite the contested election result, George W. Bush came to office with a rather stable public image, largely viewed as personable, honorable, decisive, and straightforward and as a man of "faith." As a result of the attacks of 9/11, Bush was immediately viewed as a strong and decisive leader. However, as the confrontation with Iraq grew, Bush was beginning to be portrayed in the press as being arrogant, closed minded, and judgmental primarily because of his faith. His continued talk of faith, the power of prayer, and America's special place in the purposes of God made many Americans uncomfortable, not to mention many leaders and citizens across the globe. Throughout Bush's campaign for reelection, religion became a major issue of public discussion and debate. Just what is the proper role of religion in positions of public leadership and decision-making? Indeed, why did "moral values" become the primary issue of voter influence in the 2004 presidential campaign? What is the relationship between "moral values" and public leadership?

Today, as never before, we need to select *moral* leaders, leaders of character and integrity. Franklin Roosevelt called the presidency "preeminently a place for moral leadership."[3] We should actively seek those who reflect the very best of personal and public values. Our expectations for public leaders should exceed those of the private sector. A president is more than a manager. Leadership is more than words. *Moral presidential leadership* instills trust, confidence, and more active, reflective citizenship. *Moral presidential leadership* is essential to a healthy republic and a democratic form of government.

Let me also be very clear from the outset: there is no doubt that we all are "moral" failures by any criteria of measurement. When we look at the moral failures of others, of course it is appropriate to retort, "There, but for the grace of God, go I!" Of course, I too have sinned and will continue to do so. However, I'm not running for president. Few stand to serve as president of the United States. For those special few who seek the office, we must demand not perfection, but traits, qualities, and behaviors that reflect honesty and integrity. At the very least, we should use the Clinton historical episode(s) as a teachable moment for the future of the republic. This endeavor is not about scoring points with conservatives or Republicans or bashing Clinton. As president, Clinton was alarming, and there are important lessons to be learned.

For example, the Monica Lewinsky scandal was about more than sex. Fundamentally, it was about public and private lies, breaches of public trust and confidence, and, quite simply, criminal behavior. The episode was just one of several in the life of Bill Clinton that is about judgment, public trust, illegal conduct, and the role model of the highest public elected official in the world. And what about George W. Bush? Was or is he a good antidote to Bill Clinton in terms of honesty, integrity, or being a role model? In comparing the two, do "moral values" play any role in our governance, for better or worse?

ETHICS AND OUR NATIONAL CHARACTER

Since the beginning of time, humans have expressed a concern for ethics. Plato's *Republic* is essentially a work of political ethics, as is Aristotle's *Nicomachean Ethics*. For both Plato and Aristotle, the "good" person was a conscientious citizen contributing to the city-state. The notion of civic virtue implies a citizenry that is informed, active, selfless, enlightened, and, above all, just.

Life today is more individualistic. We are concerned with self-actualization, "success," comfort, convenience, property, and the pursuit of happiness. For more than a decade, there have been increasing numbers of studies, polls, and news articles lamenting the decline of ethical behavior in America. As early as 1987, the cover of *U.S. News & World Report* asked, "A Nation of Liars?" and *Time* magazine, "What Ever Happened to Ethics?" *Atlantic Monthly* in 1992 and *Newsweek* magazine in 1995 explored the absence of a "sense of shame" as a norm in our culture. Lying and cheating among adults and among our children have become rather commonplace. More recent surveys show that 80 percent of high school students admit to having cheated at least once, with half stating they did not believe cheating was necessarily wrong. In fact, many indicated that it is necessary to lie, cheat, or steal in order to succeed. Even 54 percent of middle school children admit they have cheated on an exam. Ninety-two percent of high school age children report that they regularly lie to their parents.[4]

The numbers for college students are equally disappointing. Seventy-five percent of college students admit to cheating. As of the summer of 2002, there were well over 300 Internet term paper sites offering essays on thousands of subjects, even offering to write custom papers for an exorbitant fee. During this time frame, a poll conducted by Zogby International revealed that 73 percent of college students agreed with the statement that "what is right and wrong depends on differences in individual values and cultural diversity" versus the 25 percent who believed that "there are clear and uniform standards of right and wrong by which everyone should be judged." Two percent were not sure.[5]

Sadly, the same general disregard for ethical behavior can be found among the general public. A national poll revealed that 30 percent of individuals admit to putting extra work experience or educational experience on their resumes; 40 percent, telling someone that "the payment is in the mail" when actually it isn't; and 55 percent, lying about their age in order to get a special discount, to name just a few examples.[6]

According to Michael Josephson of the Josephson Institute of Ethics, "we have become desensitized to the enormous significance of lying. The effects are all destructive, generally lowering the level of trust in anything we read or hear."[7] The cumulative effect is to give everyone permission to lie because, most certainly, the powerful do so.

In the summer of 2001, a Gallup poll found, for only the second time in fifty years, ethics and morality near the top of the list of most important problems facing this nation. Seventy-eight percent thought our moral values are "somewhat" or "very weak."[8] It seems the nation is in an ethical slump.

We ended the twentieth century "praising" a president who was impeached, ultimately disbarred, and found in contempt of court for lying under oath, not to mention to the American public. We began the twenty-first century with the largest number and scope of corporate scandals and transgressions since the years before the Great Depression.

Should presidents ever lie? Of course we want our leaders to be of high integrity, but we also want our presidents to be capable of being adroit, tough, perhaps even ruthless if necessary. There have been occasions when presidents have lied to us that may well be justified. For example, Dwight Eisenhower lied twice as president: once in 1944 to Hitler about where Allied forces were going to invade and once on May Day to Khrushchev about what Francis Gary Powers was doing in the U-2 aircraft over the Soviet Union. Thus, lying to foreign governments may be necessary in order to protect American lives or secrets.

The fragmented nature of society today makes defining ethical behavior more difficult. We separate our world into personal, business, political, and religious realms. We approach each realm with a different set of behaviors. The segmentation can be an excuse to ignore ethical behavior appropriate in one context if we're operating in a different realm. We might find lying to our spouse completely unacceptable but could soften the stance on lying if talking to a supervisor. Deception and fraud abound in society across all occupations and socioeconomic groups. Individuals from the fields of entertainment, business, politics, and others too numerous to list are frequently in the news as a consequence of acts of deception. These examples don't remove the responsibility of conducting ourselves in an ethical manner, but they offer abundant rationales if we're looking for an excuse.

It also seems we live in a time of shamelessness. Cheating in business, in politics, and in education is commonplace. One can cheat, lie, or steal and do so profitably. Examples abound:

- Disgraced journalists writing books about their misdeed and profiting from them.
- Young people downloading and sharing music files, thinking this is not stealing.
- Corporate executives living extravagant lifestyles while aware that their money was obtained fraudulently.

Along with this time of shamelessness, there is the lack of public outrage. As a sense of shame becomes less common, and the sense of individualism rises, we come to care less about what others think. There seems to be a public willingness to ignore bad behavior if it is entertaining. Perhaps our current decline of moral behavior and outrage is linked to today's desire to succeed quickly at any cost. What's more, evil deeds will more likely gain notoriety and fame. Note Monica Lewinsky and her new line of handbags; Jayson Blair, reporter from the *New York Times* who plagiarized and fabricated material, then ended up on the covers of both *Newsweek* and *New York* magazines proclaiming a lucrative book contract; or Stephen Glass, who made up stories for the *New Republic*, publishing a novel of the experience.

In the past, one was shunned for misdeeds. With shame, Richard Nixon and Gary Hart literally disappeared for years from public view. Today, a shameful act is a good way to gain attention, perhaps even get your own radio or television show! Arkansas governor Mike Huckabee speculates that there is almost a desire among today's public to witness the character and integrity failures of public officials. Why? Governor Huckabee thinks that "by showing the character flaws in other people, the public affirms that its own inadequacies are really not so abnormal. As the character of America begins to plummet, we want to justify our own lack of morality by somehow showing that everyone is just as bad."[9]

Historically, there has always been great skepticism about the practice of politics and, above all, about politicians. In many public opinion polls, politicians rank below car salespeople and attorneys as the most dishonest profession. Part of the problem is the continual string of "bad" actions of many politicians, beginning, some argue, with the resignation of Richard Nixon, and including the allegations of sexual misconduct in office by former senator Gary Hart and most recently Bill Clinton, to name only a few instances that generate concern among voters.

Some ethical dilemmas arise because of the difference between campaigning and governing. George H. W. Bush's reversal of his pledge not to raise taxes in 1992 was portrayed as an act of willful deception and outright lying, not as an act of leadership and conscience. Some scholars attribute his reversal as a major reason for his defeat in 1996. As another example, some citizens question the veracity of George W. Bush proclaiming Iraq's holdings of "weapons of mass destruction" as justification for going to war against Saddam Hussein. In addition, during the presidential campaign of 2000, George W. Bush proclaimed that America should not participate in "nation building."

Other concerns are raised about the actual process of getting elected. Many citizens assume that politicians will say or do almost anything to get elected. For many, the critical question becomes whether ethical politics is possible or whether the notion is simply an oxymoron.

As you will come to learn, I think we, as citizens, are as much at fault as the individuals we have perhaps poorly chosen to serve our nation. The qualities of honesty, integrity, and trust between leaders and citizens are fundamental to a healthy democracy. Without undertaking a detailed philosophical discussion of democracy, one can identify several critical characteristics of a democratic form of government that are relevant to this discussion. The notion of accountability is essential to the notion of democracy. Because citizens delegate authority to those who hold office, politicians are accountable to the public for all actions and deeds. Elections are just one method of accountability. In America, news journalism serves as another check on political power and authority. The "watchdog" function is a long-standing tradition of the American press. *Information* is critical for citizens to make informed judgments and evaluations of elected officials. Naturally, incomplete or inaccurate information can lead to bad public decisions. A *free marketplace of ideas* is vital to a thriving democracy. Diversity of thought and respect for dissent are hallmarks of the values of freedom and justice. When multiple viewpoints are heard and expressed, the "common good" prevails over "private interests." Finally, democracy is a process of what Dennis Thompson calls *collective deliberation* on disputes of issues and fundamental values.[10] It is the national and public debate that determines the collective wisdom and will of the people. Thus, personal ethics are fundamental to democracy.

PRESIDENTIAL CHARACTER

From my perspective, there is simply no better way of choosing a candidate for president, especially in today's complex and dangerous world, than by evaluating what kind of human being the candidates really are. I fully concur with Robert Shogan that "any understanding of the presidency has to begin with understanding of the relationship between presidential character and presidential performance."[11] He succinctly argues, "The strengths and weaknesses of presidential character help shape presidential performance for good and for ill . . . character is a double-edged sword—an instrument that can discredit presidents and destroy their credibility but also one that presidents can use to establish their political identity and mobilize support. In sum, character, combined with values, is the ultimate weapon in modern American politics."[12]

The character of each president, from George Washington to the current George W. Bush, not only influences public policy but also impacts the institution of the presidency. With George Washington in mind, the framers granted the chief executive rather unique powers. Washington's character and self-discipline instilled trust that as president, he would not take advantage of or abuse power. By even staying a second term while preferring to return home, he held the country together when there were bitter political divisions at home and abroad. By leaving when he did, Washington demonstrated that no one is indispensable nor did we need a monarch.[13]

According to Shogan, the presidencies of greatest impact upon the office succeeding Washington until the modern presidency period of post–Franklin D. Roosevelt include Jefferson, Jackson, Lincoln, Theodore Roosevelt, and Woodrow Wilson.

Jefferson's character established the political style of presidential leadership. By bolstering his appeal to the mass electorate, Jackson's character reshaped the presidency into a far more democratic design than the Founding Fathers imagined. Lincoln's character, dominated by his commitment to reason, helped him save the union and give a new dimension to the political creed born with independence. As the nation entered the twentieth century, Theodore Roosevelt's gift for self-dramatization laid the foundation for the media presidency, and for America's new imperial role as a great power. Woodrow Wilson, the moralist who led the country into the Great War, sought to give that power a conscience and a global mission, the nature of which would divide his countrymen for generations to come.[14]

As a "dual-edged sword," character traits can do harm and have unintended, even somewhat subtle, influences. Even the greatest strengths of presidential character may also turn out to be the source of their greatest vulnerability.

Truman, in manner, demeanor, and stature, suffered in comparison to Franklin D. Roosevelt. However, according to Shogan, it was his very ordinary, common "everydayness" of behavior that provided the key to his character. Truman's greatest asset was that he understood his strengths and weaknesses. "An honest man, at peace with himself, relatively free from inner torments, he was able to make the most of his abilities."[15] Truman's childhood was challenging, with near blindness and small stature. In addition, his family was broke while he was growing up and he never attended college. Upon his return from World War I, Truman failed in several businesses. His legislative record was modest, at best. He was a "safe" and "compromising" choice for vice president. However, as president, he was strong, courageous, and straightforward. Truman made the decision to use the atomic bomb, removed popular General MacArthur, and never gave up in his reelection bid of 1942. Truman's character is reflected in every decision he made, and history is kind to him.

Dwight Eisenhower is an interesting case. He was not elected because of his political beliefs or ideology. Eisenhower was elected because of his character and popular personality. The campaign slogan "I like Ike" sums up his appeal. Ike's skills of leadership were not based solely on his self-confidence, but also on simply getting along with others, teamwork, persuasion, and reasonable goal-setting. His presidency reflected the mood of the times, one of stability rather than one of change.[16]

John Kennedy brought a sense of change and movement to the presidency. Enter the age of the politics of charisma and of television. Kennedy's character, above all, was based on ambition, to win in endeavors large and small. Not particularly ideological, fairly moderate compared to today's understandings of liberal and conservative, Kennedy, like

Eisenhower, ran primarily on his personality. Despite his slim margin of victory, Kennedy wanted to inspire the nation: to reach the moon and to bring democracy to the world. His actions were bold, but less than successful: the failed invasion at the Bay of Pigs, the near nuclear exchange over the Cuban missile crisis, and the buildup of forces in Vietnam. Much of Kennedy's public persona and heroic image was based on the love affair with the press at the time. He provided them access, cute stories, a sense of humor, and a dramatic life story. We now know a very different presidency, one of constant sexual escapades, chronic back pain, Addison's disease, strong daily medication, and macho displays. "Privately and publicly, Kennedy lived and governed at the edge."[17]

Lyndon Johnson's character was based on pride and ego, resulting in most issues being reduced to elements of personal competition. To "win," Johnson would use strategies ranging from flattery to direct bullying. He worked best one-on-one, personal and private. Johnson's legislative legacy is impressive. However, in the end "it was because of his inner conflicts that he did not make any honest decision at all. As a result, the Great Society crumbled, and Vietnam turned into the first war the United States ever lost."[18]

Of all the contemporary presidents, most Americans readily admit to the faulty character of Richard Nixon. After thirty years, he is still characterized as introspective, vindictive, defensive, paranoid, ill tempered, and moody. Although he proclaimed, "I'm not a crook," we came to understand that he was a liar. According to Shogan, Nixon's "greatest character strength was that he could make himself do almost anything he felt needed to be done to make his way in the world."[19] Throughout his career, Nixon found himself in confrontation after confrontation. His will and determination as character strengths for most of his life led to political disaster during his presidency. Nixon became a polarizing president. The legacy of Watergate, as we will discuss in subsequent chapters, forever changed the institutional presidency.

Gerald Ford was known for his loyalty and personal integrity. However, it was his sense of loyalty and aversion to confrontation that led to his decision to grant Nixon a presidential pardon. This decision would be decisive in his run for the presidency in 1976. The pardon, just four weeks into his presidency, renewed public cynicism and speculation that Nixon's resignation was in exchange for a full pardon. In actuality, the pardon reflected the genuine personal thoughts and convictions of Ford. Politically, it damaged the good he generated in his presidential transition and became a problem in his bid for the office.[20]

Consider, as another example of character traits serving as a "dual-edged sword," Jimmy Carter. Throughout his campaign of 1976, he proclaimed that he was a born-again Christian and promised to never tell a lie. Carter's sterling character traits were well received in the shadows of the Johnson and Nixon presidencies. However, Carter's strong moral foundation and values generated rigidity of thought, purpose, and policy that resulted in what some would call a failed presidency.

Consider also Ronald Reagan, who was so successful in communicating his positive personality and strong beliefs. Reagan came across as sincere, genuine, and extremely likeable. But his somewhat relaxed management style ensnared him in the Iran "arms for hostages" deal that tainted his presidency.

As we recall, George H. W. Bush neither had the gift of being a strong communicator nor possessed very strong convictions. Interestingly, in his 1988 race against Michael Dukakis, instead of evoking his own values of character, the Bush campaign attacked Dukakis's values. Dukakis was portrayed as outside mainstream America, short on patriotism, indifferent to the working class of everyday Americans, soft on crime, and, above all, simply a Northeastern liberal.[21]

Shogan claims Clinton largely dismissed the issue of character during the 1992 presidential campaign. When questioned about the importance or role of character in presidential campaigns, Clinton responded, "The people whose character and patriotism is really an issue in this election are those who would divert the attention of the people, who destroy the reputations of their opponents and divide the country we love."[22] After all, what is private is no one's business and, essentially, "what we don't know won't hurt us." Such rationale must be rejected for obvious as well as for subtle reasons. Again, consider an interesting observation by Shogan: "The fact that Warren Harding, who led America in the Roaring Twenties, had a mistress, means little by itself. But the mistress's revelation made after Harding's death that their relationship reflected Harding's obsessive need for approval and affection might have served as a warning of the scandalous corruption that ultimately engulfed a president who would not separate himself from his crooked friends because he feared being without any friends."[23]

THE INSTITUTIONAL PRESIDENCY AND LEADERSHIP

Certainly in the last twenty-five years we have seen a transformation or a transition in terms of the roles and functions of the American presidency, not so much from a constitutional perspective, but from a cultural/sociological one. My focus is on the presidency as a social institution, as it interacts with the public and the public with the institution.

Public expectations and perceptions are created through presidents' rhetoric, use of symbols, rituals, and sense of history. In essence, the office is created, sustained, and permeated through interaction comprised of campaigns, socialization, history, and myth. Certainly, from a public perspective, the presidency is a very different office since the Nixon era. Watergate led to a fundamental reappraisal of the beliefs about the presidency and its role in American democracy.

The presidents of the postwar era have certainly not enjoyed political good fortune despite the "power" and "majesty" of the office. Of the ten presidents of this era, from Harry Truman to Bill Clinton, two declined to run again because of unpopular wars, one was assassinated, two survived assassination attempts, two faced the possibility of impeachment and conviction, one was impeached, three failed to be elected as incumbents, and, despite public job approval ratings, President Clinton enjoyed the lowest personal character rating of any president since such polls were taken. In short, we witnessed the transformation of the American presidency from the heroic leadership model of governing to a more managerial model of governing, from a parental model of leadership to a CEO model of management.

Presidential scholar Barbara Kellerman argues that conceptions of leadership and management have converged as we enter the twenty-first century. Leaders in the business community have become more similar to those in government or politics in terms of activities, skills, and demands. She predicts that as we go forward into this new century, leaders will move from business into politics, and from politics into business, more easily and frequently.[24]

Leadership as a concept is many things: a process, a product, a method, a style, a group of behaviors or skills, to name just a few approaches. Rather than focusing on the content of leadership, reflect on how presidents lead. Presidents lead by words, deeds, action, and the symbolic vestments of the institution. By words I mean public discourse. By deeds I mean their specific legislative agenda. By action I mean personal character, personality, and habits of behavior. By the symbolic dimensions of the office, I mean the historical, mythic, public expectations of the institution. These components, that is, words, deeds, action, and symbolic dimensions of the presidency, generate a public impression, or orientation to the occupant's management style.

For example, some scholars have identified the Nixon administration as the "imperial presidency" based primarily upon his deeds (a rather aggressive legislative agenda) and his use of the symbolic attributes of the office. The Ford administration may be characterized as the "caretaker presidency" based upon deeds (a rather modest legislative agenda) and action (his personality and habits). Charles Jones has provided a convincing argument characterizing the Carter administration as the "trustee presidency" with Carter relying primarily upon the leadership components of deeds (an expansive legislative agenda) and action (his personal character and job personality).[25] While the Reagan presidency is most often called the "symbolic" or "heroic presidency," across both terms he relied upon all four components of leadership of words (public discourse), deeds (legislative agenda), action (personal character, personality, and habits), and the symbolic dimensions of the office. President George H. W. Bush has been characterized as a "bargainer" relying on deeds (legislative agenda) and action (personal character, personality, and habits). Finally, Clinton is the great "compromiser," relying upon primarily words (public discourse) and deeds (legislative agenda). Thus, in very simplistic terms, Nixon was the imperial president, Ford the caretaker, Carter the trustee, Reagan the heroic president, George H. W. Bush the bargainer, and Clinton the compromiser.[26]

Notice that presidents may utilize the same components of leadership but generate very different outcomes of success and public images. While Reagan was most successful utilizing the symbolic aspects of the office, it was one of Nixon's downfalls. Carter and George H. W. Bush enjoyed personal support based upon character and personality (i.e., action), but were judged deficient by the public on elements of competency and effectiveness (i.e., deeds). You will note that in my judgment, Ronald Reagan was the only president of those mentioned to attempt to use all four components of presidential leadership. President Clinton, because of his personal scandals, lost the viability of using the components of action and the symbolic majesty and authority of the office. The dynamics and implications of these elements will become clear in subsequent chapters.

CONCLUSION

Three fundamental questions drive the following analysis. Does character matter in the presidency? Did the Clinton administration foster the public's confidence in our government or encourage continued erosion of the public's trust in our leaders and government? I believe it has done the latter. Finally, what is our role in selecting presidents worthy of our trust and confidence in office?

In terms of ethics and the Clinton administration, Gregory Walden observes: "First, the White House has conducted itself often as if it were oblivious to ethics concerns, taking action without regard to whether ethical restrictions exist or whether the action would give rise to improper appearances. Second, the White House has compiled a consistently poor record of responding to ethics controversies, exacerbating rather than mollifying the public's suspicion of wrongdoing. Third, in these and other matters, the President and White House have displayed a fundamental lack of candor—a repeated unwillingness or inability to tell it straight."[27]

Political scientists and historians are just now beginning to ask the questions: Where was the public outrage for Clinton's behavior? Why didn't the impeachment of Clinton shake the country? Why did the public generally support Clinton putting us through such an embarrassing and revealing process? Just what is the legacy of the Clinton presidency? Is George W. Bush an antidote to the Clinton presidency? What do we want and/or need in our presidents?

As the first post–Cold War president, first of the new global economy, and more importantly, the first of his baby-boomer generation, the Clinton presidency will be the reference point for all the presidents that follow. This is certainly the case for George W. Bush. When considering Clinton and the scandals and impeachment as related to the presidency, there are legal, political, constitutional, and institutional concerns. The primary concern here is the institutional, social meaning of the office of president of the United States of America and how the occupant impacts the polity well beyond the constitutional powers and obligations of the office.

NOTES

1. James Bovard, *"Feeling Your Pain"* (New York: St. Martin's Press, 2000), 1.
2. Bovard, *"Feeling Your Pain,"* 4.
3. Robert Shogan, *The Double-Edged Sword* (Boulder, CO: Westview, 2000).
4. Glen Altschuler, "Battling the Cheats," *Education Life*, January 7, 2001.
5. http://www.zogby.com
6. Carolyn Kleiner and Mary Lord, "The Cheating Game," *U.S. News & World Report*, November 12, 1999.
7. Karen S. Peterson, "High-profile Fibs Feed Public Cynicism," *USA Today*, July 5, 2001. http://www.usatoday.com/news/health/2001-07-05-lying.htm, retrieved June 30, 2004.
8. Peterson, "High-profile Fibs Feed Public Cynicism."

9. Mike Huckabee, *Character Is the Issue* (Nashville, TN: Broadman & Holman, 1997), 91.
10. Dennis Thompson, *Political Ethics and Public Office* (Cambridge, MA: Harvard University Press, 1987), 3.
11. Shogan, *The Double-Edged Sword*, xi.
12. Shogan, *The Double-Edged Sword*, 3.
13. Shogan, *The Double-Edged Sword*, 31.
14. Shogan, *The Double-Edged Sword*, 36–37.
15. Shogan, *The Double-Edged Sword*, 93.
16. Shogan, *The Double-Edged Sword*, 98–102.
17. Shogan, *The Double-Edged Sword*, 118.
18. Shogan, *The Double-Edged Sword*, 128.
19. Shogan, *The Double-Edged Sword*, 133.
20. Shogan, *The Double-Edged Sword*, 139–43.
21. Shogan, *The Double-Edged Sword*, 10.
22. Shogan, *The Double-Edged Sword*, 10.
23. Shogan, *The Double-Edged Sword*, 5.
24. Barbara Kellerman, *Reinventing Leadership* (Albany: State University of New York Press, 1999), 208.
25. Charles Jones, *The Trusteeship Presidency* (Baton Rouge: Louisiana State University Press, 1988).
26. It is too soon to provide such a characterization for George W. Bush.
27. Gregory Walden, *On Best Behavior: The Clinton Administration and Ethics in Government* (Indianapolis, IN: Hudson Institute, 1996), 5.

The Diminished Presidency: Post-Clinton

To sin by silence makes cowards of all men.

—JOHN ASHCROFT

As a child, I was always very interested in presidents and the presidency. I would read biographies and histories of our great leaders. From my grandparents, I would inquire about Franklin Roosevelt, Harry Truman, and Ike Eisenhower. In grade school, my book reports and history papers were always on some president. Later, in college, I would write as many papers as possible dealing with some aspect of the presidency.

The first presidential candidate I ever met was Jimmy Carter. I was an undergraduate student at Wake Forest University. Having endured the Nixon presidency and the Vietnam War, I was captivated by the message of this largely unknown candidate for the presidency. When Carter spoke, it was a message of hope, faith, and confidence in the American people. His speech that evening was structured around several rhetorical questions. Can our government be as honest, decent, open, fair, and compassionate as the American people? Can our government be competent? Can our government in Washington represent accurately what the American people are or what we ought to be? And he concluded by asking, "Why not the best?" I left the event that evening with a copy of his book *Why Not the Best?*, a gold peanut lapel pin, a handshake, and a sense of commitment to his campaign. As a fellow Southerner, I shared pride in his candidacy.

However, I came to be disappointed in his presidency, but not in the man (although some of his statements post-9/11 and during the current "war on terror" have caused me some concern). Nearly a decade ago, I was fortunate to meet President Carter once again and to have several moments of private conversation. I wore the gold peanut lapel pin he had given me nearly twenty years earlier. He immediately recalled his Wake Forest visit, the importance of defeating George Wallace in the North Carolina presidential primary, and the excitement of the campaign. I left the event that evening with a sense of admiration, pride, and appreciation for his service. Overall, he is a good man, a great individual who served our nation well. Although perhaps disappointed in his performance as president, I was never embarrassed.

For me, the Clinton presidency is one of disappointment and embarrassment. Other administrations have had ethical lapses. But the sheer number and extent within the Clinton administration makes it one of the worst. It was, after all, Clinton who promised in 1992 to have one of the most ethical administrations in history. Instead, it has been one of the most investigated.

Consider just a part of the legacy of the Clinton administration:

- Only president ever impeached on grounds of personal malfeasance
- Greatest number of convictions and guilty pleas by friends and associates
- Greatest number of cabinet officials to come under criminal investigation
- First president sued for sexual harassment
- First president accused of rape
- Hillary as first of all first ladies to come under criminal investigation
- Largest criminal plea agreement in an illegal campaign contribution case
- First president to be found in contempt of a federal court
- First president to establish a legal defense fund
- Greatest amount of illegal campaign contributions

Among the crimes for which convictions and plea agreements have been obtained from Clinton and associates are perjury, obstruction of justice, money laundering, illegal campaign contributions, fraudulent loans, fraud, conspiracy, tax evasion, racketeering, extortion, bribery, and drug trafficking, to name just a few.

In the words of Stanley Renshon,

How was it possible for a president who consistently lied to the public and to his own administration; who was found guilty of perjury for lying under oath while testifying in a civil suit and before a federal grand jury, and who in both cases was guilty of obstructing justice; who personally orchestrated the most massive stonewalling effort since Watergate to keep the truth of his inappropriate behavior from the public; who was believed by the public to have committed the offenses for which he was impeached; and whose behavior would not be tolerated in any CEO, professor, military commander, or anyone in a position of power and responsibility nonetheless manage to maintain high levels of public approval throughout his and our ordeal?[1]

Other questions come to mind. Do we no longer care about the honesty and integrity of our presidents? Do personal character and values no longer matter?

In the wake of the Clinton sex scandals and administrative investigations, as discussed in some length in the last chapter, Americans continue to struggle with the role and importance of personal character and morality in public life. Despite our prosperity, declining rates of crime, and relative world peace prior to the attacks of 9/11, for more than a decade, there continues to be a general uneasiness about the deterioration of American culture. Members from both the left and the right, although for very different reasons, lament the drift away from traditional values.

The Lewinsky scandal was not about sex. It was clearly about public and private lives. It was also about breaches of public trust and confidence, not to mention criminal behavior. The facts are simple and indisputable. William Jefferson Clinton lied to his wife, to his daughter, to the American people, to his closest aides, to members of his cabinet, and to members of the grand jury. Therefore, the Lewinsky "issue" was not *just* about private sex. It was about judgment, public trust, illegal conduct, and, yes, the role model of the highest public elected official in the world.

Understand the historical significance of the situation. From Washington to Bush, no sitting president had ever been indicted for a criminal offense. Remember that Nixon was named as "coconspirator." Clinton was the first president to be impeached. No president until Clinton has been fined resulting from being held in contempt of court. No sitting president was sued to lose his license to practice law (although Nixon was disbarred after office in New York).

Bill Clinton's repeated betrayal of public trust has a profound impact on our political and civic culture. For Barbara Olson, "the Clintons created a tabloid presidency that blurred the differences between the *National Enquirer* and the *New York Times*."² He contributed to the debasement of language and brought sex into virtually everything. Just what constitutes "sex"? And how interesting to learn on national television from Robert Bennett, Clinton's attorney, that the president's genital organ was of "a normal man" in terms of "size, shape, direction."³

From a political perspective, Clinton, quite simply, diminished the institutional presidency. His administration contributed to the continued decline and trust of government and elected officials. Without trust, presidents may win office, but they cannot effectively govern. The problem is not one of legality, but of legitimacy. When citizens become less trusting, it makes it difficult for future presidents to restore trust. Despite reliable third-party and congressional testimony about the lack of quality of information about Iraq and weapons of mass destruction, many Americans and noted politicians called George W. Bush a liar during the 2004 presidential campaign. "Ultimately," as Stanley Renshon observes, "the fabric of democracy is in danger as the psychological adhesive that holds it together loosens."⁴ The simple lack of candor throughout Clinton's term speaks to the genuine failure of his administration in terms of public leadership.

THE DECLINE OF TRUST IN GOVERNMENT

There has been an obvious decline of the public's trust in government. Since 1958, the University of Michigan's Survey Research Center has tracked how much the public trusts the government in Washington to do what is right. This annual survey confirms the suspicions that Americans are losing confidence in their government, especially under Bill Clinton. In 1958, 78 percent of the public said they could trust government all or most of the time. The numbers stayed at that level until the second year of Lyndon Johnson's administration, dropping to 69 percent. By 1976, the number had fallen to 35 percent. During the Reagan years, the numbers were in the low 40s. However, by the 1992 presidential campaign, only about 23 percent thought the government could be trusted to do what's right all or most of the time. After two years of the Clinton presidency, the number was only 18 percent.⁵ In fact, Arvind Raichur and Richard Waterman found a consistent pattern of declining presidential approval ratings since 1953.⁶ Public distrust of government weakens citizen connections to public life and results in less interest in public affairs, lower voter turnout, and cynicism.

I suspect not only that there is long-term damage to the office but that the spiral of citizen participation in the life of the nation continues to decline. What is more alarming to me, we have a generation of Americans now going to college who grew up with Clinton as president. He was primarily the first "leader of the free world" they witnessed in office. I was unnerved by the jokes of my teenagers and saddened by the lack of respect for the office and the occupant. I was embarrassed by discussions of oral sex and other "presidential activities" reported during newscasts. There was even a pornographic film made about the "Clinton/Lewinski episodes" by Arrow Productions (1998) entitled *Deep Throat V: Slick Willy Rides Again* complete with look-alikes playing the various roles. How much of today's cynicism and the notions of politicians were formed from the turmoil of Nixon and Watergate? What will be the cost of the Clinton scandals on my children and grandchildren of the future? Will the best and brightest of the next generation aspire to be president? For the right reasons?

Just as violent video games and rap music impact children, so too does the behavior of leaders and role models. If, as Hillary Clinton advocated, "it takes a village to raise a child," then it also takes members of the "village" to set moral and ethical examples of leadership for future generations. If we, as parents, don't want our children to behave irresponsibly, to lie, to deceive, then how can we rationalize Clinton's behavior? Clinton did just about everything that a parent would advise against: lying, cover-ups, disloyalty to friends and family, and displays of selfishness. Yet our impressionable youth saw how we as a nation turned a blind eye to the scandals and unacceptable behavior.

"Make no mistake," as David Schippers concludes, "the conduct of the President is inextricably bound to the welfare of the people of the United States. Not only does it affect economic and national defense, but even more directly, it affects the moral and law-abiding fiber of the commonwealth, without which no nation can survive."[7]

Now, at the beginning of the new millennium, what would a survey of our social and political landscape reveal today? As one who has studied and written about American politics and political campaigns for more than twenty years, I am alarmed, concerned, and even saddened by our political climate and attitudes reflected in our society today. There exists among the public a climate of change, a climate of distrust, and even a climate of fear. And on all levels of measurement, Americans participate less and are less concerned and interested in affairs of state.

For example, recent studies tell us that young people can no longer identify public heroes. A quick review of major public opinion polls of

2004 and 2003 reveals general public cynicism and distrust of government. Only 23 percent of Americans have a great deal of confidence in the presidency, 11 percent in Congress, and 16 percent in the Supreme Court.[8] Only 27 percent think you can trust government to do what is right "most of the time."[9] Sixty-four percent of Americans think Congress cannot fix anything. Since 1966, the Harris polling organization has asked a series of questions resulting in what they call the "Alienation Index." The lower the total number, the less citizens feel alienated from government. The first index stood at 29. By 1971 it had risen to 40, and by 1977, because of Watergate and the Vietnam War, it rose to 59. In 1991 it was 66, and it reached the highest point ever in 1995 at 67.

The index fell to 55 in 2000 and to 47 in 2001, even after the attacks of 9/11. However, the index went up to 52 in 2002 and for 2003, the last year currently available, up two points to 54. In fact, according to the 2003 Citizen Alienation Index, 67 percent of Americans think people in Washington are out of touch with the rest of the country, 54 percent think people running the country don't care what happens to them, and 60 percent think people in power will try to take advantage of everyday citizens. Between 1990 and 1999 there was only one year in which the index fell below 60. The average alienation score for the 1990s was 63, compared to the 57 average score during the 1980s.[10] Perhaps the most alarming statistic reported during this same time frame is that 74 percent of Americans think the American Dream of "equal opportunity, personal freedom, and social mobility" will be harder to achieve in the next ten years!

But what about today's college students? Nationwide, only 33 percent of those eighteen to twenty-four years old voted in the 2000 presidential election, one of the closest and most contentious elections in modern American history. This low turnout rate is part of a twenty-five-year trend of decline, ever since 1972 when eighteen-year-olds were first permitted to vote. Since that time, overall turnout has declined about 4 percent. However, for the eighteen- to twenty-four-year-olds the decline has been 15 percent, or on average 31 percent lower than the adult voter turnout rate.[11] A report published in March 1999 by the National Association of Secretaries of State revealed that those between the ages of eighteen and twenty-four want to help their communities by volunteering and raising their children well, but have very little interest in the political process and voting. In the study, the highest priorities of young people were having a close-knit family, developing job skills, and having a successful career. Alarmingly, the lowest-rated priorities were being a "good American" and being involved in democracy and voting.

Perhaps such attitudes explain why in 1996, Americans conducted a presidential campaign that resulted in the lowest national turnout since 1924 and in which less than half of registered voters participated in the defining act of democracy. Even on election night, network ratings were the lowest ever recorded by Nielsen in an election year. Just 39 percent of homes with television viewed election night returns.

The 1998 midterm congressional elections reflect the same degree of low interest among Americans. The national turnout rate was just 36 percent of those eligible to vote, the lowest level since 1942. In the 2002 midterm races, once again only 36 percent participated. At least in 2004, turnout was up across all constituent groups, primarily given a time of war and international terrorism.

"Anger" was the political watchword of the 1990s. Academic and civil leaders continue to write about the absence of civility, the decline of intelligent dialogue, rising decibels of hate speech, and increasing "nastiness" of political campaigns. The unifying theme behind the social anger of the 1990s was *government*. Government, in many ways, had become the scapegoat for all that we perceive to be wrong within our society.

Ironically, in the aftermath of winning the Cold War, the political climate became one of public distrust, cynicism, and even fear. Why have so many Americans lost confidence in their government and trust of elected officials and politicians? A 2000 NPR/Kaiser/Kennedy School poll provides some insight. Government waste and inefficiency was identified by 73 percent, partisan bickering by 68 percent, too much influence by special interests by 65 percent, and *a lack of honesty and integrity among elected officials* by 64 percent.[12] Government and the political process are viewed as dominated by special interests rather than notions of the "common good" for all Americans. Many citizens feel caught in the crossfire of self-interested politicians, special interest groups, and large corporations, all lacking basic integrity. In 1995, Francis Fukuyama wrote that Americans were experiencing a genuine "crisis of trust."[13]

Presidential leadership reflects a set of relationships between presidents and citizens. In general, the public cedes power to make decisions based upon implicit and explicit understandings. It is assumed that the president will act in the public interest, not self-interest. It is assumed that the president will be honest with the American people and provide debate and information to support decisions. Finally, it is assumed that presidents will use the powers of the office in reasonable, responsible, and competent ways.

Robert Spitzer argues that Watergate was a transformative moment for the institutional presidency that extended well beyond Richard Nixon:

"It ended the century-long march toward an ever-stronger presidency, but because it altered the nature of the imperial presidency debate and legitimized the wariness of executive excess."[14] For William Berman, Clinton's impeachment "continued the long-term loss of presidential prestige that began with Lyndon Johnson's presidency."[15]

PRESIDENTIAL LEADERSHIP

How important is the office of president to our society? Is it equal to the clergy? Is it equal in importance to the leaders in our military? Do we expect higher personal and ethical standards from law enforcement officers? Is it reasonable for a congregation to dismiss pastors for unethical or inappropriate conduct, personal or private? Is it inappropriate to dismiss a police officer who has broken the law? Is it unfair to expect military officers to follow a strict code of personal conduct? In terms of social leadership, should we expect less from the president of the United States?

Management is about expertise. Leadership is about judgment and making decisions. The exercise of judgment expresses elements of character, experience, wisdom, and vision. Presidential judgment allows assessment of presidential performance. So, what do we make of Bill Clinton as president? One must go beyond the individual to the importance of the office itself within the context of our nationhood.

The very foundation of this nation is about values, ideals. It is not about the "economy, stupid." The vast majority of the signers of the Declaration of Independence were wealthy individuals, at the top of the social ladder. Yet they risked it all. Many lost everything. It was the promise of freedom, individual responsibility, and democratic self-rule that captured the hope of the Founding Fathers. The Declaration of Independence and our Constitution provide the moral framework and justification for our government and society. They are not just simply operational manuals.

Beyond the questions of individual fitness for office is the larger issue of how we define politics in America. Of course presidents of questionable personal character have served successfully and those of the utmost qualities of integrity have been less than effective in the office. My purpose is not to analyze the role of good character in terms of presidential performance. I am concerned about *good people* serving this nation. Although I am not concerned about private behavior per se, in terms of the presidency, there is no such thing as private behavior.

I fear that the notion of genuine presidential greatness may be gone. In the words of Michael Genovese, "We live in an age of failed leaders. . . . As circumstances call for leadership, we may instead get pandering and petty rankling."[16] For the generation between John Kennedy and Bill Clinton, the reputation of the American presidency has been in decline. G. H. Bennett observes, "One cannot help but be struck by the contrast between perceptions of presidential power at the time of Watergate in the 1970s, and in the aftermath of the publication of the Starr Report in 1998. The apparent decline is cataclysmic, and the shifts in public and academic perception are remarkable."[17] While acknowledging that the presidency has long provided American political culture with its dominant image of leadership, Bruce Miroff posits that the image generated of the heroic presidency by midcentury no longer seems believable in America: "At century's end, the image of the energetic executive appears exhausted. . . . The exhaustion of the presidential image, then, is a story of mounting disbelief."[18]

For Miroff, the heroic imagery of the presidency began to collapse with the twin disasters of Vietnam and Watergate. In addition, Jimmy Carter did the most to fuel academic discussions of presidential weakness. "Constrained, confined, limited, deflated—these were the kind of terms through which the heroic image of presidential power lost its hold over presidency scholarship."[19] J. T. Young predicts that Clinton will be remembered as a "small man in small times" who reduced the dominant role the presidency has played since 1933. "This deliberate diminution of the presidency is unprecedented in post–World War II American history. Ironically, it may also serve to be Clinton's greatest legacy, however unwittingly it came about."[20]

More than a decade ago, Suzanne Garment proclaimed, "Welcome to American politics after Watergate, in which survival counts as a victory, public servants are busily perfecting the art of government by Post-It note," and there is an ever-present "scandal-hunting press corps."[21] Three of the six past incumbents lost their bids for reelection and six of the past seven presidents left office in disappointment or under less-than-desirable circumstances.

Today's rise in public alienation is fed by incessant scandal, and our mistrust has created political habits and institutions that now continue to produce more mistrust and cynicism. This culture of mistrust makes the job of governing measurably more difficult. Ultimately, we largely view the political leadership of our country with contempt. Bennett agrees with Garment that "superior campaign machines, rather than superior candidates, were what seemed to turn presidential elections, and the emphasis on personality had become a beauty contest where the best cosmetics won the day."[22]

After two hundred years of confidence and stability, in the 1990s the office became the center of great controversy and debate. Unfortunately, for many Americans, the office has become largely irrelevant, even in our world, post-9/11, of terrorism. The issue is not that we will never have great presidents again or even good ones, for as presidential scholar Aaron Wildavsky observes, "Presidents come and go but the presidency lives on."[23] The problem is in the relationship of the office with the public and symbolic vestments that seem to have been squandered. Of course, the diminution of the presidency has its roots in presidential performance across the last forty years.

Thus, especially during the 1960s and 1970s, the United States passed through a tremendous internal political crisis that drained the nation's energy, taxed its patience, and threatened its constitutional system. Good intentions, inflated promises, and a commitment to action failed to solve the problems. Under the banners of the New Frontier, the Great Society, the New American Revolution, WIN (Whip Inflation Now), "a shining city on the hill," and the New Covenant, presidents pledged major innovations and social change. Each also generated, however, a grievously large gap between promise and performance. In general, it appears the public voted for activism in 1960, for peace in 1964, for tranquility in 1968, for competence in 1972, and for some form of change in 1976, 1980, and 1992.

THE POSTMODERN PRESIDENCY

For some scholars and political observers, Clinton ushered in the "postmodern presidency," "where the organizing themes of modern American politics—the heroic presidency, the Cold War, the conflict between Democratic liberalism and Republican conservatism—are superseded by fleeting images and issues that do not produce any consistent or coherent political understanding."[24] In this era, "postmodern character" refers to "a political actor who lacks a stable identity associated with ideological and partisan values and who is, thereby, free to move nimbly from one position to another as political fashion dictates."[25]

According to Shawn and Trevor Parry-Giles, "postmodern" American politics is dominated by "the image" and a "hyperreal" depiction of candidates and leaders. Such politics largely rejects historical norms and expectations of leadership. Postmodern politics "simultaneously rejects and embraces existing presidentialities while it seeks to craft a new presidentiality for a hyper-mediated, hyper-visual, hyperreal time."[26] As a result, following their analysis, "Voters and citizens are constructed as more targeted, more fragmented, more scopophiliac, more skeptical than ever before. They are repeatedly told that their political system does not work, that their leaders are dishonest and solely motivated by money and special interests, and that little or nothing can be done to solve intractable problems facing the nation. They are also conditioned to believe that politics is artificial, and they long for a real, genuine, authentic politics, as if such a community has ever existed or will ever be possible."[27]

Given this "postmodern environment," poor Clinton is portrayed by many academics as simply a victim of contemporary politics. For example, the Parry-Gileses posit that Clinton was forced to confront the impact of the "ghosts of Nixon, Johnson and JFK." As the argument goes, Clinton embodied not only the angst related to the presidency but also the larger cultural tensions inherent in his generation. As the first baby-boomer president, he was forced to deal with the "ambiguity, confusion, and irony" associated with such issues as the Vietnam War, the military draft, drugs, casual sex, divorce, and so forth. "Thus, even as Clinton uttered his first words on the campaign trail, even as he took the oath of office, his bid for the presidency as well as his performance in office were shaped by the ideological dissonances of the larger political culture."[28]

A major Clinton apologist, journalist Joe Klein, concurs with the Perry-Gileses. "It seems likely, in retrospect, that Bill Clinton was a compendium of all that his accusers found most embarrassing, troubling, and loathsome about themselves, especially those who come of age, as he did, in the deep, narcotic prosperity that enveloped the nation after World War II. On the most superficial level, his excesses reflected the personal excesses—sexual and material—of his generation."[29] Of course, we all reflect the values, mores, and culture of our times. However, in terms of public leadership, we must seek and elect the best of our generation.

The institution of the American presidency is a paradox. The office always seems too strong or too weak. A president appears to have too much power for the realization of "self-rule" while lacking enough power to solve this nation's most critical problems. The American public, as the story goes, wants a common man in the White House but expects uncommon leadership. The public demands that a president be above "politics" while forgetting that to be elected an individual must be, above all, a politician. By acting decisively, the president is labeled "dictatorial" and "unconstitutional." But by failing to act decisively, the president is called "passive" and "weak." Why has such a paradoxical institution survived for more than two hundred years?

Part of the answer lies in the fact that the institution is largely undefined. The Constitution is alarmingly vague on the responsibilities, dimensions, and roles of the office. I would posit that the office has survived and functioned well primarily because of its fundamentally symbolic nature. Presidential historian Thomas Cronin argues that one of the overriding functions of the president is "to provide symbolic affirmation of the nation's basic values and aspirations."[30] Yet, because of the historical and continued excesses and abuses, many Americans question the integrity of the office and have become increasingly cynical about the moral authority of the institution. At most, increasingly Americans simply want a manager, a CEO to run the country.

CONCLUSION

Since the founding of the nation, Americans have nearly always favored solving problems by reforming structures. Increasingly, it is becoming clear that structures are only a small part of the presidency. Structures, in fact, are arranged by individuals with unique perceptions, beliefs, and attitudes that play a significant role in the ultimate uses of those structures. In addition, they exist in a cultural context consisting of specific norms and expectations. Hence, the current "problems" of the modern presidency and the nature of the office go beyond the constitutional-legalistic questions, the institutional organizational charts, the pressures of economic elites or interest groups, the specialized "inputs" and "outputs" of policy, and the "real" personality of individual presidents.

Virtually every American, from seven to seventy, has a list of criteria of what makes a "good" president. Yet, when consulting the ultimate authority, Article II of the Constitution, which delineates the functions and duties of the president, one notices how short, sketchy, vague, and almost trivial the description of the office appears.

Although the presidency is indeed a very real office with an elected official, space, desks, and staff, it remains elusive and undefined. Historically, the presidency is the work of the presidents. Expectations are created through presidents' rhetoric, use of symbols, rituals, and sense of history. From the beginning of the nation, Americans are taught at home, in the schools, and in pervasive political rhetoric that America is the land of equal opportunity, that there is equality before the law, that government accurately reflects the voice of the people, and that political and economic values are allocated fairly. Within such an environment, as Clinton Rossiter notes, the president becomes "the one-man distillation of the American people," reflecting their perceived dignity and majesty.[31] Consequently, elaborate criteria are envisioned for the person who desires the "sacred" office.

It was important for presidential candidates to try to conform to the public expectations of goodness and fairness. By being "one of us," the president should naturally reflect the qualities comprising the "average American citizen" perpetuated in the myth of the "American character."

Historically, a candidate was helped by being perceived as trustworthy, reliable, mature, kind but firm, a devoted family man, and in every way normal and presentable. But these attributes alone are not enough. Americans also require a sense of direction and strength. Oftentimes, the president serves as our interpreter of the past and our linkage to the future.

The institution of the American presidency is greater than any individual. The office greatly influences the officeholder, who must conform to already established expectations of presidential performance and behavior. The sets of expected presidential roles result from the historic interaction of the office with the public. Public perceptions and expectations influence, mold, create, and restrict the presidency as well as presidential behavior. The role sets are created, sustained, and permeated through social interaction comprised of campaigns, socialization, history, and myth. The presidency, as an institution, has important consequences on public behavior.

As members of the republic, we must not lower our expectations of leadership nor give our leaders a "pass" when they fail to perform or meet our expectations. I am well aware that nearly a majority of those who voted in 1996 returned Clinton to the White House. My concern is that too many Americans have lowered their expectations of presidential performance and behavior. We seem to ignore the value of the historic or symbolic dimensions of the office. We should not lower our expectations of leadership. Indeed, if we lose the appreciation for the historic and symbolic aspects of the office, we will lose its most valuable asset.

NOTES

1. Stanley Renshon, "The Public's Response to the Clinton Scandals, Part 1," *Presidential Studies Quarterly*, 32 (1), 2002, 169–84.
2. Barbara Olson, *The Final Days* (Washington, DC: Regnery, 2001), 207.
3. Olson, *The Final Days*, 108.
4. Stanley A. Renshon, *High Hopes: The Clinton Presidency and the Politics of Ambition* (New York: New York University Press, 1996), 257.
5. Renshon, *High Hopes*, 29.
6. Arvind Raichur and Richard Waterman, "The Presidency, the Public, and the Expectations Gap," in *The Presidency Reconsidered*, Richard Waterman, ed. (Itasca, IL: F. E. Peacock, 1993), 17.
7. David Schippers, *Sellout* (Washington, DC: Regnery, 2000), 244.
8. Gallup poll, May 21–23, 2004, PollingReport.Com, http://www.pollingreport.com/institut.htm, retrieved July 1, 2004.
9. *Newsweek* poll, October 9–10, 2003, PollingReport.Com, http://www.pollingreport.com/institut.htm, retrieved July 1, 2004.

10. HarrisInteractive, December 31, 2003, http://www.info@harrisinter active.com, retrieved July 1, 2004.

11. Peter Levine and Mark Lopez, "Youth Voter Turnout Has Declined, by Any Measure," Center for Information and Research on Civic Learning and Engagement, University of Maryland, September 2002, http://www.civic youth.org, retrieved July 1, 2004.

12. NPR Online, "Americans Distrust Government, But Want It to Do More," July 28, 2000, http://www.npr.org, retrieved June 30, 2004.

13. Francis Fukuyma, *Trust: The Social Virtues and the Creation of Prosperity* (New York: The Free Press, 1995).

14. Robert Spitzer, "The Presidency: The Clinton Crisis and Its Consequences," in *The Clinton Scandal and the Future of American Government*, Mark Rozell and Clyde Wilcox, eds. (Washington, DC: Georgetown University Press, 2000), 4.

15. William Berman, *From the Center to the Edge* (Lanham, MD: Rowman & Littlefield, 2001).

16. Michael Genovese, *The Presidential Dilemma* (New York: HarperCollins, 1995), ix.

17. G. H. Bennett, *The American Presidency: 1945–2000* (Gloucestershire, UK: Sutton Publishing Limited, 2000).

18. Bruce Miroff, "From 'Midcentury' to Fin-de-Siecle: The Exhaustion of the Presidential Image," *Rhetoric & Public Affairs*, 1 (2) (1998), 186, 188.

19. Miroff, "From 'Midcentury' to Fin-de-Siecle," 190.

20. J. T. Young, "Clinton in Context," *Currents in Modern Thought*, January 2000, 327.

21. Suzanne Garment, *Scandal: The Culture of Mistrust in American Politics* (New York: Anchor Books, 1991), 2.

22. Bennett, *The American Presidency*, 244.

23. Aaron Wildavsky, *The Beleaguered Presidency* (New Brunswick, NJ: Transaction, 1991), xv.

24. Bruce Miroff, "Courting the Public," in *The Postmodern Presidency*, Steven Schier, ed. (Pittsburgh: University of Pittsburgh Press, 2000), 106.

25. Miroff, "Courting the Public," 106.

26. Shawn J. Parry-Giles and Trevor Parry-Giles, *Constructing Clinton* (New York: Peter Lang, 2002), 5.

27. Parry-Giles and Parry-Giles, *Constructing Clinton*, 15.

28. Parry-Giles and Parry-Giles, *Constructing Clinton*, 158.

29. Joe Klein, *The Natural* (New York: Doubleday, 2002), 184.

30. Thomas E. Cronin, *The State of the Presidency* (Boston: Little, Brown, 1975), 4.

31. Clinton Rossiter, *The American Presidency*, Revised edition (New York: Mentor Books, 1962), 16.

3

The American Presidency: The Job Description

The executive power shall be vested in a President of the United States.

—CONSTITUTION OF THE UNITED STATES,
Article II, Section 1

The presidency, as an institution, does indeed respond to the laws of Darwin. The institution is ever evolving and changing. Despite the constitutional provisions of 1787, forces inherent in American society have transformed the office created by the framers into the unique institution it is today. Too often, the "scientists" of politics search for indisputable data, measurable elements, and clear decisions of the office. Yet, the presidency is more than the product of data analysis. Indeed, the presidency is a product of interaction. The institution is comprised of the public's historic, mythic perceptions and expectations of the office. It "grows" as individual occupants and situations mold, shape, create, and reinforce various public perceptions and expectations of the office. The presidency is not what goes on behind closed doors. Its true significance and impact lie in its public domain. The American political system is not simply a historical structure. Rather, it is a composition of people and becomes a social object that is selectively conceptualized, interpreted, and reinforced as a result of the interaction of people within the structure.

The informal and symbolic powers of the presidency today account for as much as the formal ones. In so many ways, the modern presidency has virtually unlimited authority for nearly anything its occupant chooses to do with it. In other ways, however, our beliefs and hopes about the presidency very much shape the character and quality of the presidential performances. As Bruce Buchanan notes, the evaluation of presidents is in the context of American political culture.[1]

THE CONSTITUTIONAL JOB DESCRIPTION

Article II of the Constitution, dealing with the presidency, is, at best, vague and sketchy. In fact, of all the major clauses in the Constitution, the one governing the presidency is the shortest. The members of the Constitutional Convention did not delineate in great detail the powers and responsibilities of the presidency. According to presidential scholar Clinton Rossiter, eight key decisions were made at different times throughout the convention that created the form and structure of the American presidency:[2]

1. A separate executive office should be established apart from the legislature.
2. The executive office should consist of one man to be called the president of the United States.
3. The president should be elected apart from the legislature.
4. The executive office should have a fixed term subject to termination by conviction of impeachment for high crimes or misdemeanors.
5. The president should be eligible for reselection with no limit as to the number of terms.
6. The president should derive power from the Constitution and not simply from Congress.
7. The president should not be encumbered with a specified body to seek approval for nominations, vetoes, or other acts. And
8. As president, one may not be a member of either house of Congress.

These "key" decisions created the office, but they contain little information as to what the office entails. Nearly half of Article II simply deals with tenure, qualifications, and election of the president. A content analysis of Article II of the Constitution reveals that the major concern of the Founding Fathers was the process of selecting a president. Forty-six percent of the words deal with the provision of the election of a president.

The next largest percentage of verbiage was dedicated to the presidential appointments. Overall, just 38 percent of the words explicitly deal with the enumerated powers of the presidency.[3]

Section 2 of Article II states that the president "shall be Commander in Chief," "shall have power to grant reprieves and pardons," "make treaties, provided two-thirds of the Senators present concur," and "appoint Ambassadors, other public Ministers and Consuls, Judges of the Supreme Court, and all other officers of the United States . . . by and with the advice and consent of the Senate," and "shall have power to fill all vacancies that may happen during the recess of the Senate." Section 3 adds that the president "shall from time to time give to the Congress information of the State of the Union," "convene both Houses . . . on extraordinary occasions," "receive Ambassadors and other public Ministers," and "take care that the laws be faithfully executed." These, then, are the duties as specified in the Constitution. On the surface, they appear rather simple and straightforward. It is the fulfilling of these functions that empowers or complicates the office. From this brief discussion of presidential functions, the Constitution as a job description is vague and general. A president clearly "does" more than what is outlined in the Constitution.

Presidential scholar Edward Corwin was the first to mention presidential roles as sources of power.[4] A president's power is based upon five constitutional roles: chief of state, chief executive, chief diplomat, commander in chief, and chief legislator. These roles are roughly analogous to the various areas of responsibilities outlined in the Constitution. A president who creates additional roles and hence additional power approaches a dangerous "personalization of the office."

As chief of state, the president functions as the ceremonial head of government, not unlike the monarchy of England. Some would argue that the majority of presidential activity is ceremonial. Projected upon the president is the symbol of sovereignty, continuity, and grandeur.

As chief executive, the president is manager of one of the largest "corporations" in the world. Whether presidents like it or not, they are held responsible for the quality of governmental performance ranging from a simple letter of complaint to military preparedness.

In event of war, the president, as commander in chief, must ensure strategic execution and victory. Within modern history, the field of foreign relations has become extremely important and primarily the domain of presidential discretion. The formulation of foreign policy and the conduct of foreign affairs force the president to serve as the nation's chief diplomat.

Finally, by providing domestic leadership, the president must guide Congress by identifying national priorities for legislation. These "legitimate," constitutional roles are obviously interrelated. Yet the various "hats" require rather distinct approaches, strategies, and temperament. Even these, however, may be situational.

Clinton Rossiter, building on Corwin's analyses, argues that five extraconstitutional roles must be recognized: Chief of Party, Protector of the Peace, Manager of Prosperity, World Leader, and Voice of the People.[5] Rossiter, like Corwin, believes that the source of presidential power lies in the combination of the various roles. Rossiter, at least, recognizes the "expanding" nature of the presidency. These extra roles resulted from the growing activities of a president plus the growing expectations of the public. Expanding roles become obligations and duties.

PRESIDENTIAL EXPECTATIONS

Certainly, the American presidency has established a rather clear traditional role set. Historically, the tendency of Americans is to believe in great personages. Within our society, the presidency fulfills a parental role and becomes the symbol of our hopes. Until the last couple of decades, presidents were more likely to be placed on a "pedestal" than under a "microscope."

As already mentioned, there appears to be a growth in public expectations of the presidency. Twentieth-century presidents, because of the use of mass media, have encouraged the public to identify with the candidate and potential of the office. Consequently, the public has responded by holding the president accountable for meeting various demands. There are two general types of expectations that citizens have of political leadership. Diffuse support focuses on the office, and specific support focuses on the individual who holds the office.

In terms of diffuse support, an individual president is the embodiment of our nation. Each citizen identifies the president with his or her own private and particular notion of what this nation is and what Americans are. If this is true, one may further argue that there are as many different specific expectations of presidential performance as there are citizens, because no two citizens share the same visions of national being or national destiny.

Without doubt the president is the best-known American political figure. The office has strong emotional and psychological attachments for Americans. Fred Greenstein, for many years, notes the profound emotional response of most Americans to the office.[6] Indeed, the death of a president generates "somatic symptoms" of personal distress. The National Opinion Research Center reported that, in light of the Kennedy assassination, 43 percent of Americans experienced loss of appetite for more than four days, 48 percent reported insomnia, 25 percent headaches, 68 percent general feelings of nervousness and tenseness, and 26 percent rapid heartbeats. Similar responses were noted in deaths of presidents Lincoln, Roosevelt, McKinley, Garfield, and "even Harding."[7]

Generally, most presidential scholars, although using somewhat different terminology, believe that the American people expect four major aspects of presidential behavior. First, the president is expected to be a competent manager of the vast machinery of government. Second, the American people expect the president to take care of their needs by initiating programs, proposing legislation, and safeguarding the economy. Third, a president is responsible for our national security, to protect our national borders and interests around the world. Finally, the people want a sense of legitimacy from the president. The office, while providing symbolic affirmation of the nation's values, should faithfully represent the opinions of the public as well. As will become clear in subsequent chapters, Clinton, in my opinion, fails in at least two of the four expectations.

In terms of specific personal characteristics, what type of person should be president of the United States? What qualities should one have for the job? Scholars and citizens alike have confronted the issue. Indeed, judgment is required at least every four years. Simple surveys easily produce a "laundry list" of desired presidential qualities, a very demanding list to be sure. However, with the Clinton administration, Americans seemed to alter the list in drastic ways.

Rossiter, once again in his classic work, identified seven qualities "that a man must have or cultivate if he is to be an effective modern President."[8] First, a president must have bounce: "that extra elasticity, given to few men, which makes it possible for him to thrive on the toughest diet of work and responsibility of the world." In addition, the presidency demands affability, political skill, cunning, a sense of history, the newspaper habit ("must be on guard lest be cut off from harsh reality"), and a sense of humor. Such qualities, I am sure, are indeed needed. I also think they would be an asset for any corporate CEO or other executives.

Emmet Hughes, in his classic entitled *The Living Presidency*, also of a "white knight" orientation believing in a "heroic presidency," prefers to address qualities that "[shape] and [make] an effective Presidential style."⁹ Such a style includes:

1. A sense of confidence; "with no harm to his leadership so grave as a show of hesitation."
2. A sense of proportion; "the avoidance of excess and extravagance."
3. A sense of drama; "a truly important Presidency has never failed to raise the noise and dust of combat."
4. A sense of timing; "sure instinct for pace and rhythm."
5. A sense of constancy; "With no necessary loss of popular trust, he may vary his methods, but he must not appear to vary or to waiver."
6. A sense of humanity; "humility and humor, and toward the people, with warmth and compassion."
7. A sense of perspective; "no saving quality that a President may lose more swiftly upon entering the White House."
8. And, above all, a sense of history.

Such an approach is more profitable. It provides more of a guideline for presidential performance than a list of specific qualities.

What can be surmised from such diverse lists of desired presidential qualities? First, for many Americans they are largely "useless" and naïve. The qualities may be characterized as admirable, often contradictory, general, abstract, and even "biblical." Some would argue they have no direct relationship to job or task performance. Despite the historical notations of such personal character expectations, the question becomes whether the public imposes these qualities on the president or whether presidents create the impressions of meeting these qualities. Clearly, the answer is both. As a result of the interaction, when presidents "appear" to meet the desired qualities, then the qualities become embedded as part of the public's expectations. Finally, the desired qualities often reflect individual senses of "goodness," "morality," and "right" and "wrong." Individuals may occasionally drink but be appalled at such behavior from their ministers. Consequently, it is not surprising that the public desires presidents not to do as the citizens do, but to do what they say to do.

There is no test that presidential candidates take to reveal true intelligence, integrity, a sense of history, and so forth. They are simply forced to demonstrate through campaigning that they, in fact, are intelligent, honest, or knowledgeable. Hence the qualities are in the minds of the citizens and largely depend upon "perception" as to their reality.

What is the impact of these historic, public expectations upon the institution? It is here that we begin to see the erosion of confidence in the office of the presidency. We begin to understand why Americans have become disenchanted and even cynical about the power and potential of a national leader. For thirty years now, the mainstay of presidential scholarship is based on the "expectations gap thesis"—the idea there is a gap between what the public expects of its presidents and what presidents actually accomplish. Especially during campaigns, they promise more than they can deliver.[10] Indeed, my very first book back in 1982, entitled *The Symbolic Dimensions of the American Presidency*, was such a treatise. Unfortunately, as the argument goes, the difference between what some of us imagine the presidency to be and what it really is leads to disappointment, frustration, and attack. Thus, expecting the impossible from a president inevitably leads to disappointment in performance.

But disappointment in presidential performance is not the only consequence of false expectations. They also encourage presidents to attempt more than they can accomplish in any term of office. Thus, false expectations invite presidents to overpromise and overextend themselves. This, in turn, creates the need for image-making activities. Such activities, in some cases, become the major task or work function of an administration. Soon, the emphasis, out of necessity, becomes style over substance.

Especially since the Carter administration, the public-relations apparatus not only has directly enlarged the presidential workforce, but also has expanded public-relations expectations about the presidency at the same time. More disquieting is the fact that, by its very nature, this type of press-agentry feeds on itself, and the resulting distortions encourage an ever-increasing subordination of substance to style and policy debate by sound bites. Diane Heith claims that the Clinton administration was more obsessed with polls than any previous presidency. The administration used polling to test policy options, speech phrases, and terms and, above all, to design a political strategy to survive the impeachment process.[11]

THE PARADOXICAL NATURE OF THE AMERICAN PRESIDENCY

The net result of this cycle is what political scientists refer to as "the paradoxical nature of the American presidency." Simply stated, the public's historic expectations and demands of the presidency invite paradoxical, two-faced behavior. As presidents attempt to please everyone, their behaviors are often contradictory and even appear schizophrenic.

There are ten rather distinguishable paradoxes of the American presidency. In terms of leadership, we desire a president to be moral and decent, yet in a time of crisis we demand forceful and decisive action. If the situation demands it, the nation will immediately applaud toughness and even ruthlessness.

Also related to leadership, the president is required to be both programmatic as well as pragmatic. Presidents are elected, theoretically, based upon proposed programs; yet, once in office, we expect the president to be flexible and open to changing demands. The most comfortable position, therefore, appears to be on the fence. The trick is to be specific but not too specific. Campaigns are exercises in winning elections, not in education.

More recently, a major theme of presidential campaigns is "innovative leadership." Candidates are expected to have future visions, plans, and goals for the nation. But should public opinion become the chief guide for leadership in America? To solve this dilemma, a president must show that indeed the architectural plans of the future are desired by the majority. This is achieved through persuasion utilizing various means.

Interestingly related to the above point, Americans seem to enjoy inspirational, "grand" rhetoric but are indeed becoming more suspect of "pie in the sky" solutions. Programs such as the "New Deal," the "New Frontier," the "Great Society," the promise of "a new covenant," and "compassionate conservatism" raised hopes and optimism about the course of the nation as well as the future. But, as already argued, as promises have more frequently failed, the public's outrage increases—until another election year.

Increasingly, we want an open, cooperative, and sharing president while also applauding courageous, daring, and independent presidential behavior. As a nation, secrecy is deplored, yet some of the best "actions" this nation has ever undertaken were shielded with secrecy.

One of the most interesting paradoxes of the office is the desire of most Americans for the president to be "nonpolitical" and to make "nonpartisan" decisions. Yet in order to be elected and reelected, a president must be a skillful politician. While being "above politics," presidents must also function as head of their party and cultivator of political sanctions. The chief executive, unlike many, functions as a monarch, prime minister, and party head. Each of these roles, at certain times, creates advantages for certain groups at the expense of others.

Equally interesting is the distinction between what it takes to become president and what is required to govern the nation. A good campaigner may not be a good administrator. Running for president requires ambiguity, style, and image. Governing requires mechanistic, concrete, and workable solutions. Many scholars point to Jimmy Carter as a contemporary example. In 1976, he ran an almost-perfect campaign. The image and issues espoused hit a very responsive note among the people. Once elected, however, he encountered an unresponsive bureaucracy and an uncooperative Congress. As a result, the passage of "innovative" programs and routine oversight of national concerns were indeed difficult. As the election year of 1980 approached, Carter's critics became more vocal about his lack of managerial capabilities. Indeed, the nation denied Carter a second term.

Part of the broad "American dream" is the belief that any citizen may become president of the United States. We prize the notion of a "common man," one of "us" providing leadership for the citizenry. Yet, once presidents are elected, we demand uncommon leadership, great insight, and vast knowledge from them. However, by the end of the Clinton administration, it seems, we simply gave up on such notions. Clinton was, indeed, too common as a representative of his baby-boomer generation. Journalist Joe Klein recognized the shift. "Clinton may have lost a great deal of his moral authority well before Lewinsky by snuggling too close to us—by polling every last public whim, by trying so hard to please. It is entirely possible that the Clinton era will be remembered by historians primarily as the moment when the distance between the president and the public evaporated forever." Our leaders have become followers.[12]

Finally, perhaps the greatest paradox of the office is in relation to its perceived power. Depending upon specific individuals and situations, the presidency is always either too powerful or not powerful enough. The president should "take care of" something or "keep out" of an affair. The president, in one situation, should take all measures necessary to control inflation yet should not interfere with wages or prices of goods. As a nation we are quick to call for decisive action and equally quick to yell "foul."

The presidency is a focus of feelings and exists solely in the minds of individuals. As James David Barber observes, "the White House is not the President any more than the flag is the nation."[13] The presidency is merely a collage of images, hopes, habits, and intentions shared by the nation, which legitimizes the office and reacts to its occupants. Politically, most Americans know little about the workings of Congress or the Supreme Court. But in terms of the presidency, the American people "respond" rather than simply "react" to the office. At one time, the president was the one symbolic figure upon which rested the hope for the nation's future. Every presidential candidate at least attempts to be so.

THE SYMBOLIC PRESIDENCY

Over the last twenty years, Americans in general have less concern and tolerance for politics. Indeed, we tend to expect "government" to deal with complex problems, generate solutions, and provide rationales for action. "People for whom politics is not important," argues Murray Edelman, "want symbols and not information: dramatic in outline, devoid of detail and of the realistic recognition of uncertainties and of opposing consideration."[14] The importance of this notion, in terms of the presidency, is the fact that the office is public property. The presidency truly "represents" more than the office "does." The nation may tire of a specific individual but not the institution. What Bruce Buchanan noted in the late 1970s would certainly be true today in terms of the Clinton administration: "The traditional Presidency has burrowed deeply into the American psyche and sparked there a visceral and abiding trust in the institution—a trust that apparently cannot be destroyed by an occasional miscreant President. Indeed, the hold of the historical Presidency on the minds of the people may well be the single most important reason for the political stability that distinguishes this government from most others."[15]

No other institution singularly spans the nation and encompasses the scope, intensity, frequency, and probability of impact as does the presidency. The American presidency is the most conspicuous office in the world. By reputation it is also the most powerful office on Earth. Domestic crises are followed throughout the world. Presidential comments and behavior are regularly reported in most foreign nations.

From a national perspective, one function of leadership is to create appropriate political settings that may legitimize a set of values. The assumption is, of course, that control over the behavior of others is primarily achieved by influencing the definition of the situation. In a democracy, the secret is to act in such a way that creates an image of the actor or scene that leads others to act voluntarily as desired. Although such attempts at "impression management" are frequent and the mainstay of contemporary politics, they certainly are not new. In 1928, W. I. Thomas wrote, "If men define situations as real, they are real in their consequences."[16] Getting others to share one's views of the world is the first step toward getting others to act in a prescribed manner. Creating or defining "reality" for others best achieves desired behavior. In turn, the use of potent symbols, rituals, and myths is useful in creating "commonalities" in the midst of national diversity. The interrelationship of these factors is succinctly described by Dan Nimmo: "By inducing people to respond in certain ways, to play specific roles toward government, and to change their thoughts, feelings, and expectations, significant political symbols facilitate the formation of public opinion. As significant symbols of political talk, the words, pictures, and acts of political communicators are tip-offs to people that they can expect fellow citizens to respond to symbols in certain anticipated ways."[17]

Individual appropriate behavior becomes societal, mass appropriate behavior. Presidential persona needs are created; expectations of performance are sustained and permeated, and consequently affect individual and mass behavior. Communication scholar Walter Fisher argues that within the images of the presidential persona lies a part of each of us. For this reason, moving the nation toward specific action can be fairly easy. Images of the presidents are "symbolic[;] they not only depict the President, they also imply an image of us; we respond to the implied image of us in relation to our self-concept; and the degree to which the implied image and self-concept correspond determines the degree to which we will believe and follow a President."[18]

The entire process, however, yields more than desired behavior. Soon, the process becomes a commitment and total belief in the institutions and system of government. As the myths, images, and symbols are sustained, so too are commitment, loyalty, and behavior. Although political symbols, myths, rituals, and talk are all rather commonplace, their implications upon behavior are significant although subtle. Walter Fisher, once again, provides a succinct way to appreciate the symbolic presidency: "It should be borne in mind that the Presidency is an office and a role, an institution and a persona. At one and the same time, it is symbolic suasory force, a source of inducement to belief, attitude, value, and action; it is a dramatic place, a stage for conflict between heroes and villains, a ground for myth, ritual and legend; it is obviously a position of power and governance; it is a focal point of national reason and rationality; and it is a barometer of public morality and an instrument of humane and inhumane policies."[19]

Every situation in which the president is a part becomes an elaborate drama. Even a news conference earmarks a dramatic performance in contrast to information sharing, where reporters are part of the setting and become instruments for influencing impressions and opinions. All drama is powerful in the sense that it influences cognition, perceptions, and hence expectations of presidential performance or behavior.

Political leadership refers to the relationship that exists with the public. In terms of this discussion, one should recognize the importance of "symbolic leadership." Often, the real appeal of public officials is what they symbolize rather than what they have done.

Symbolic leadership is an emergent phenomenon resulting from the interaction of the public and the politician. As political drama begins, roles are identified, interpreted, and projected upon the politician. The key, therefore, in becoming a symbolic leader is to take advantage of the dramatic elements in any setting.

The sources of images or preconceptions people have of the qualities of leadership are vast. There are, however, three major influences upon such leadership construction. First, history rather carefully characterizes past national leaders. Washington was a man of integrity (the cherry tree), determination (Valley Forge), and democratic values (refusal to be king). Lincoln was a man of patience ("preserve the union"), a man of forgiveness ("with malice toward none"), and a lover of freedom (Emancipation Proclamation). Second, television greatly contributes to the creation of leadership ideals. The open forums give the impression of being able to assess candidate qualities. Finally, leadership qualities are portrayed in dramatic programs and literature. Often voters openly compare the qualities of politicians to those of professional entertainers.

Each inauguration day, history is made, and another chapter of American history is carefully recorded during the next four years. Every detail of presidential behavior is noted and significance is attached. They are chosen to lead and consequently they are a part of us. The overlay of myth and magic on the presidency is like no other office.

Of all the political myths of the nation, historian Theodore White argued that the supreme myth is the ability of the citizens to choose the "best" person to lead the nation.[20] From this belief followed the notion that the office would ennoble anyone who holds the office. The weight of the responsibilities and duties would transform the average citizen into a superior individual, one of wisdom, insight, and a sense of duty. Thus, the presidency is a combination of symbol and reality. However, the symbolic dimensions of the office are increasingly becoming more important as the role of mass media has become both "maker and breaker" of presidents.

The presidency as a symbol or image has six characteristics. The institutional presidency is synthetic, believable, passive, vivid, simplified, and ambiguous. As synthetic, the impression of the office is carefully planned, manipulated, and created to serve a specific purpose. Details of leadership become massive strategies. The institution is believable in that it has prescribed meaning, significance, and expectations attached to the symbol.

The office is "real" and manifests criteria for each occupant. Yet the office is passive in the sense that the symbol is an "ideal," a mixture of hope, myth, and fantasy. In being believable, the office as a symbol is vivid and concrete. As the ideal, whatever its composition, becomes publicly shared, the office is "real" in its significance and consequences. However, in reality, the intricacies and complexities of the job are reduced to a few broad, general characteristics that are more readily identifiable. Symbols, as simplified, are also ambiguous, floating between imagination and reality awaiting people to fill in the gaps and thus to attach personal significance to the symbol.

Perhaps the forefathers were aware of the fact that the most practical method of unifying people was to give them a symbol that all could identify. When the symbol is manifested in a person, the efficacy and effectiveness is greatly enhanced. Clearly the president of the United States is the focal point of the political system. Every action by a president is symbolic because the president is not merely an executive but also a carrier of meaning. What the individual symbolizes to each person or group depends upon the system of interpretation of the person or group. Consequently, from the beginning to the end of the president's term in office, every action is a means by which citizens interpret life in the United States.

There are numerous symbols through which the president communicates to the public. To provide a laundry list of specific artifacts, phrases, or actions is not important. For some, whether the president wears a suit or not is important. Jimmy Carter was criticized for wearing jeans in the Oval Office. What is more important is to understand that what makes various actions of the president symbolic is the cluster of memories and associations inherent in the actions while recognizing that responses differ for different audiences.

The epitome of identifying the symbolic nature of the presidency is Taft's often-quoted description of the president as the personal embodiment and representative of (the people's) dignity and majesty. Noted presidential scholar Clinton Rossiter reflects Taft's statement in proclaiming that the president "is the one-man distillation of the American people just as surely as the Queen is of the British people."[21] The office is the symbol for justice, freedom, equality, continuity, and grandeur. The presidency, more specifically, mirrors "all that is best" about America as perceived by each citizen. In accordance, Thomas Cronin notes: "The Presidency is nearly always a mirror of the fundamental forces in society: the values, the myths, the quest for social control and stability, and the vast, inert, conservative forces that maintain the existing balance of interests."[22] Perhaps Michael Novak provides the strongest statement of the relationship of the presidency to the American people: "So far as his national actions go, they live in him. His acts are theirs. He is their persona. He is the people, not in a sense that subsumes them under him but in the sense that he is their agent, their spokesman, their image of themselves. So long as he has their confidence, its actions have legitimacy and power."[23]

It is a serious mistake, however, to view such a characterization of the presidency as passive. The very potency of the presidency as a symbol gives the office purpose and pragmatic nature. Americans expect presidents to prod and unite, as well as to provide direction and a sense of purpose. As such, the presidency fulfills the parental functions of supreme leader, guide, and teacher. It is important to note, however, that symbolic power is the precondition of pragmatic power. Much legislation and many programs have failed because they were not symbolically acceptable. The key to success, of course, is presidential leadership. Not surprisingly, the most frequent complaint about the presidency since the Vietnam War is "lack of leadership." The focus of my argument is that leadership is more than effective management.

It is in presidential elections, however, that symbolism is the most powerful and planned component. A campaign attempts to legitimize the candidate's visions and to demonstrate leadership capabilities. During an election, the nation is not a classroom but a theater, not an event but a saga competing for the symbolic centers of America. Novak describes a presidential campaign as "a contest for the souls, imaginations, and aspirations of Americans as much as for the nation's levers of power. It is also a contest between national self-images. Not infrequently citizens will vote against their self-interests, coldly and economically defined, for the sake of symbols more important to them."[24]

The symbolic significance of campaigns is interwoven with their pragmatic quest for power. One can recall when a single word or phrase has destroyed a candidate's chances (Romney's "brainwashed") or given a candidate serious trouble (McCain's attack on the "religious right"). An alarming show of personality may damage a campaign, as did Muskie's tears in New Hampshire or Nixon's rage in 1962. Symbolic violations may inhibit electoral success, as did Stevenson's marital status and Teddy Kennedy's episode at Chappaquiddick. The rich do not always win (i.e., Perot or Forbes) and the underdog just may triumph, as did McCarthy in 1968, McGovern in 1972, and Carter in 1976. Simply stated, the intangibles are many and the realm of the symbolic is important. In electing a president, "we elect the chief symbol-maker of the land, and empower him in the kingdom of our imaginations as well as in the executive office where he supervises armies, budgets, and appointments."[25]

For Novak, Americans not only elect a king, but also a high priest and prophet.[26] Together, the terms speak to the symbolic importance and influence of the office. The president is king in the sense of being the symbolic and decisive focal point of national power and destiny. The president is prophet in the sense of being the chief interpreter of national self-understanding and defining future endeavors. The president is priest in the sense of incarnating the nation's values and aspirations and expressing these through his behavior.

CONCLUSION

As noted from the outset, the informal and symbolic dimensions of the presidency account for as much, if not more, than the formal, legal ones. Thus, to define the presidency as principally a symbolic institution is not to lessen the significance and importance of the office. Rather, it emphasizes the subtle impact of the institution upon every citizen. To describe the president as priest, prophet, and king is to acknowledge the respect, expectations, hopes, and values of the American people.

NOTES

1. Bruce Buchanan, *The Presidential Experience* (Englewood Cliffs, NJ: Prentice Hall, 1978), 16.
2. Clinton Rossiter, *The American Presidency*, Revised edition (New York: Mentor Books, 1962), 72–75.
3. Richard Waterman, Robert Wright, and Gilbert Clair, *The Image-Is-Everything Presidency* (Boulder, CO: Westview, 1999), 151–52.
4. Edward Corwin, *The President: Office and Powers*, 3rd edition (New York: New York University Press, 1948), 20–23.
5. Rossiter, *The American Presidency*, 28–37.
6. Fred Greenstein, "Popular Images of the President," in *Perspectives on the Presidency*, Stanley Bach and George Sulzner, eds. (Lexington, MA: D. C. Heath, 1974), 134–43.
7. Greenstein, "Popular Images of the President," 135.
8. Rossiter, *The American Presidency*, 172–74.
9. Emmet J. Hughes, *The Living Presidency* (New York: Penguin, 1974), 107–34.

10. Waterman, Wright, and Clair, *The Image-Is-Everything Presidency*, 4.

11. Diane Heith, "Polling for a Defense: The White House Public Opinion Apparatus and the Clinton Impeachment," *Presidential Studies Quarterly*, 30 (4), 2000, 784.

12. Joe Klein, *The Natural* (New York: Doubleday, 2002), 208.

13. James David Barber, *Presidential Character* (Englewood Cliffs, NJ: Prentice Hall, 1972), 450.

14. Murray Edelman, "The Politics of Persuasion," in *Choosing the President*, James David Barber, ed. (Englewood Cliffs, NJ: Prentice Hall, 1974), 156.

15. Buchanan, *The Presidential Experience*, 159.

16. Peter Hall, "A Symbolic Interactionist Analysis of Politics," *Sociological Inquiry*, 42 (3–4), 1972, 51.

17. Dan Nimmo, *Political Communication and Public Opinion in America* (Santa Monica, CA: Goodyear, 1978), 69.

18. Walter Fisher, "Rhetorical Fiction and the Presidency," *Quarterly Journal of Speech*, 66 (2), 1980, 124–25.

19. Fisher, "Rhetorical Fiction and the Presidency," 119–20.

20. Theodore White, *Breach of Faith* (New York: Atheneum, 1975), 323–24.

21. Rossiter, *The American Presidency*, 16.

22. Thomas Cronin, *The State of the Presidency* (Boston: Little, Brown, 1975), 239.

23. Michael Novak, *Choosing Our King* (New York: Macmillan, 1974), 164.

24. Novak, *Choosing Our King*, 46.

25. Novak, *Choosing Our King*, 28.

26. Novak, *Choosing Our King*, 50–52.

4

The American Presidency and Moral Leadership

We will not survive the 21st Century with the ethics of the 20th Century.

—LEN MARRELLA

Bruce Miroff argues that moral codes that shape public expectations of presidential conduct change over time.[1] Indeed, the standard of presidential morality in the 1990s is very different than when the presidency was established. To illustrate this point, he compares what he calls "republican character" with "democratic character."

Republican character is composed of the classic qualities of courage, resolution, moderation, dedication, and control. Such characteristics are not psychological, but objective behavior subject to public judgment. Republican character was a lofty and cultural imperative. Miroff suggests this was the public's expectation of presidential leadership of the 1790s.

In contrast, the democratic character is one of the people. A president need not be *better* than us, but *similar* to us The democratic standard allows a president to be personally flawed in the private sphere as long as it does not impact job performance. "The standard of democratic character upholds a president who is perceived as effective and successful in pursuing an economic and social agenda favored by a majority of Americans."[2]

In terms of Bill Clinton, he clearly fails the test of republican character. "His conduct in the Monica Lewinsky scandal was consistently marked by the lack of self-control, the absence of honor, the exhibition of shamelessness. If republican character demands that a president be an exemplar of the highest public virtues, that he be better than most of us, Bill Clinton, to paraphrase Lloyd Bentsen, is 'no George Washington.'"[3] However, according to Miroff, the reason that polls showed the public's general lack of trust for Clinton but still supported his occupancy of the White House is that the democratic character has supplanted the republican character of the public's judgment of presidential performance.

As is clearly apparent by now, I endorse a return to the republican values of character. I know this may well seem impractical, old-fashioned, and "academically naïve." Historically, we readily recognize that many presidents judged to possess high levels of personal character, such as Ford and Carter, are also judged to have had low job effectiveness. Likewise, we know that some presidents with problematic character concerns, such as Kennedy and Nixon, are viewed as having been most effective and successful. However, I think we desperately need to have and to hold higher expectations of presidential leadership and character, especially in the current world climate.

James Kouzes and Barry Posner have studied leadership in a variety of contexts and situations for years. Through their interviews and research, they find that the *content* of leadership does not change; however, the context does change for all types of reasons: technology, world events, cultural and social demands, and so forth. Through their years of research, surveys, and interviews, they found five practices of exemplary leadership: model the way, inspire a shared vision, challenge the process, enable others to act, and encourage the heart.[4] We expect our leaders to be role models in every way. As my grandfather used to say, "I'd rather see a sermon than hear one." Leaders "lead" by inspiration, by challenging, by providing a clear direction for future actions or behaviors. By challenging the process, leaders are pioneers, taking us to new directions, new issues, and new challenges. We expect our leaders to be enthusiastic, energetic, and positive about the future. Inspiring leaders provide meaning and purpose in our lives. A leader's vision articulates goals and objectives, and communicates the beliefs and values that influence and shape the cultural and behavioral norms. The qualities of a great public leader, according to historian Stephen Ambrose, are vision, integrity, courage, understanding, the power of articulation, and profundity of character.[5] How did our forefathers perceive of the role of president?

HISTORICAL PERSPECTIVES OF
PRESIDENTIAL LEADERSHIP

There was a strong public expectation of moral public leadership in the eighteenth and nineteenth centuries. People were elected because of their past and often heroic behavior. Public service was viewed as a trust, an obligation, and an honor. By the twentieth century, management skills took priority over character. The rise of the professional politician replaced the genuine public servant. Elected office became a prize, not an opportunity. Personal power rather than genuine public service became a more powerful motive. Politics became a game, not a method or channel of service.

I think it is valuable to consider the kind of person the Founding Fathers thought should be president. Alexander Hamilton, in the Federalist Papers, number 76, suggested that any person elevated to the presidency should be "a man of abilities, at least respectable." The office requires men of "character," "wisdom," and "integrity." Indeed, the office requires "a livelier sense of duty and a more exact regard to reputation." This view was presented in opposition to members of Congress who, by the nature of that institution, would bring local biases and "prepossessions."[6]

Hamilton thought the office would greatly influence the occupant. "The sole and undivided responsibility of one man will naturally beget a livelier sense of duty and a more exact regard to reputation. He will, on this account, feel himself under stronger obligations, and more interested to investigate with care the qualities requisite to the stations to be filled, and to prefer with impartiality the persons who may have the fairest pretensions to them."[7]

However, cause for removal from office was very clear for Alexander Hamilton. In the Federalist Papers, number 65, removal is based upon "the abuse or violation of some public trust. They are of a nature which may with peculiar propriety be denominated *political*, as they relate chiefly to injuries done immediately to the society itself."[8]

James Madison wrote in the Federalist Papers, number 57, that "the aim of every political constitution is, or ought to be, first to obtain for rulers men who possess most wisdom to discern and most virtue to pursue the common good of the society; and in the next place, to take the most effectual precautions for keeping them virtuous whilst they continue to hold their public trust."

Clearly the forefathers envisioned rather specific criteria for the occupant of the office. For them, character and integrity were integral requirements for the position of leadership. The notion of character in those times included the qualities of courage, resolution, moderation, dedication, and control.[9] Inherent in our democratic belief is the ability of the whole to select one who is capable of leading us through tough times or dangerous events, who possesses the wisdom to articulate a social agenda and legislative programs, and who can serve as the ultimate model of citizenship. As Michael Genovese argues, "presidents who lead in the democratic spirit create leaders, foster citizen responsibility, inspire and empower others to assume leadership responsibilities in their communities. Democratic leaders establish a moral vision: pursue egalitarian goals; question, challenge, engage, and educate citizens; and offer hope."[10]

PRESIDENTIAL LEADERSHIP

As already noted, there is a difference between leadership and management. Management is a subset of good leadership. Generally, good leaders are good managers, but not all good managers are good leaders.[11] Management is about expertise. Leadership is about judgment. The notion of judgment implies consideration of issues of trust, fairness, and insight. The very credibility of leadership depends on its moral purpose, trust, and the hopes it engenders. Leaders are obligated and responsible for the moral environment of an office, a corporation, or even a society. Just as the more competent leaders tend to be more successful, those more morally mature will lead with higher moral reasoning and justification.

Kouzes and Posner point out that leadership practices are amoral. However, leaders who use the practices of leadership are moral or immoral. There is, by the very definition of leadership, an ethical dimension.[12] Ethics and leadership function as cause and effect. One simply cannot be an effective leader without ethical conduct.

I worked for a wonderful major general in the army. He told me one time that he could always "hire brains." Leadership is more than knowledge or management. It is a set of attitudes, skills, judgment, and, above all, behavior. And behavior reflects personal character. For him, leadership involves the full person. Leadership is more than management. Being a good politician is not the same as being a good president.

Aristotle recommended that a true student of politics must study "virtue above all things."[13] Moral virtues, such as "courage, moderation, and justice," dispose us toward good behavior. Moral virtue, for Aristotle, comes about as a result of habit. Thus, repeated "good" acts develop facilities for acting rightly in the future. From this classical perspective, the "good life" is the morally good life, and political authority is responsible for creating an environment for citizens, and hence the state, to develop themselves morally.[14]

Rabindra Kanungo and Manuel Mendonca categorize virtues into four groups. The moral virtues consist of honesty, truthfulness, decency, courage, and justice. Intellectual virtues are thoughtfulness, strength of mind, and curiosity. Communal virtues include neighborliness, charity, self-support, helpfulness, cooperativeness, and respect for others. Political virtues are commitment to the common good, respect for law, and responsible participation.[15]

Moral leadership emerges from the fundamental needs, aspirations, and values of the followers. Presidential historian Robert Dallek expresses the challenge best. "Successful presidential leadership has always relied on moral authority: a president's conviction that he is battling for the national good and public perception that he is a credible chief committed to advancing the national well-being. Few things are more destructive to a president's influence than the belief that he is a deceitful manipulator more intent on serving his personal needs than those of the public."[16]

Robert Putnam has popularized the notion of "moral capital."[17] As citizens, we make moral judgments about people, places, and institutions. When our judgments are positive, they inspire trust, belief, and allegiance that politically may in turn produce willing acquiescence, obedience, loyalty, support, action, and even sacrifice.

It is important for politicians to be seen to serve and to stand for something apart from their own self-interests. In short, they must establish a moral grounding. "This they do," according to Putnam, "by avowing their service to some set of fundamental values, principles and goals that find a resonant response in significant numbers of people. When such people judge the agent or institution to be both faithful and effective in serving those values and goals, they are likely to bestow some quantum of respect and approval that is of great political benefit to the receiver. This quantum is the agent's moral capital."[18]

Moral capital is different from mere popularity. Popularity may be based in part on moral judgment or appraisals but is more often based on other sources of attraction. Popularity may be bought, but moral capital cannot.

Leadership is essentially about relationships. And at the heart of any relationship is trust. For two decades, Kouzes and Posner have surveyed the general public to identify the characteristics of most admired leaders.

Only four characteristics continuously receive over 50 percent of the votes: honest (88 percent), forward-looking (71 percent), competent (66 percent), and inspiring (65 percent).[19] Note that trust emerges as the single most important characteristic. People want to know their leaders are truthful, ethical, and principled.

Mutual trust is the foundation of democratic government, of self-rule. John Locke viewed the special relationship between citizens and the executive as a fiduciary trust. The government as trustee incurs an obligation to act for the public good. In giving our support and trust to a leader, we the citizens bestow legitimacy upon the government and leader. Trust is given in exchange for a vote. Elections determine the object of trust, but then trust must be earned through deeds, words, legislative actions, and so forth. In general, the public cedes power to make decisions based on implicit and explicit understandings. It is assumed that the president will act in the public interest, not self-interest. It is assumed that the president will be honest with the American people and will provide debate and information to support decisions and actions. Finally, it is assumed that the president will use the powers of the office in a reasonable, responsible, and competent way.

The trustee relationship between leader and citizen implies higher standards of behavior. We all recognize there are differences among actions are that legal, ethical, and moral. Because elected officials act for others, they assume rights and obligations average citizens do not assume. In addition, for a trustee, standards of conduct are higher than those of the marketplace. Thus, Dennis Thompson asserts that actions taken by private citizens that may be permissible may indeed be criminal if done by public officials.[20]

Any discussion of leadership and higher standards of ethical behavior raises the issue of private versus public privacy and private versus public behavior. I was simply amazed by the public rationale and distinction between Clinton's private versus public behavior. For me, there is no distinction between private and public deception. At best, it is a matter of degrees, frequency, and magnitude.

George Washington certainly believed that private matters have public consequences. He wrote that "purity of morals [is] the only sure foundation of public happiness in any country."[21] Recall that Plato's *Republic* abolishes the very foundations of any private life for the guardians who must rule the state by eliminating the family and private property in order to create unity in the state.

Thompson even suggests that the privacy of public officials, elected or otherwise, *should* receive less respect than the privacy of ordinary citizens. "Public officials are not simply ordinary citizens. They have power over us, and they represent us in other ways. From these differences follows the principle of diminished privacy for public officials. . . . Because officials make decisions that affect our lives, we want to make sure that they are at least physically and mentally competent; that they do not abuse their power for private ends and are not vulnerable to the improper influence of others; and that they are likely to pursue policies of which we would approve."[22]

Arkansas governor Mike Huckabee readily acknowledges that families of ministers and those of elected officials are held to different standards and modes of conduct from everybody else. However, for Huckabee, being in the public eye is not just pretending to be one thing in public versus another thing in private. For him, there is a "difference between role-playing and role-living. Role-playing is a sham; role-living is being comfortable with who you are anytime an observer walks up to the fishbowl for a look."[23] Kouzes and Posner concur with Huckabee: "A leader with integrity has one self, at home and at work, with family and with colleagues. Leaders without integrity are putting on an act."[24]

It is also important to note that every president sets up expectations for his successors. As Marvin Olasky argues, "A president seen as having high moral character raises the bar for his successors, and the reverse is also true. A series of outstanding presidents increases the likelihood of the populace demanding another outstanding leader, and the reverse is also true."[25] For example, by the public's acceptance of Clinton's lies and other behaviors, future presidents actually have a lower standard of behavior to meet. Thus, "every president who speeds up the downward slide makes a return to earlier and higher standards more difficult."[26]

Studies have also shown that ethical conduct by leaders increases ethical conduct by followers.[27] Ethical behavior by leaders may excite admiration but also invite imitation. With ethical leadership, public cynicism decreases and public trust increases. However, Kouzes and Posner argue that over time, when we lose respect for our leaders, we lose respect for ourselves.[28] As Edmund Burke wrote, "great men are the landmarks and guideposts of the state." When guideposts misdirect, citizens who follow their leaders begin to wallow and become lost. Thus, trust is the bond that holds a democracy together: trust in government, in public institutions, in social and private relationships, among each other, and so forth.

Indeed, the public's confidence and trust provides the context in which a president initiates policy, responds to challenges, and in general governs. The more trust and confidence the public has in a president, the more latitude the president has to take action and shape policy. Bruce Buchanan identifies five historically proven advantages of high public presidential support. First, public support increases the support of presidential programs and legislation in Congress. Second, public support influences a president's ability to conduct foreign policy. Third, public popularity ensures more favorable media coverage and treatment. Fourth, strong public support increases presidential credibility within the executive branch of government as well as other segments of the Washington community. This was how Reagan was able to influence the notion of smaller government, less regulation, and so forth. Finally, the very strength and enthusiasm of public support generates more self-confidence and effectiveness of presidential performance.[29]

Stanley Renshon argues that an individual president does not have to change history to have an impact. In fact, the institutional importance of the office guarantees *social* significance. The combination of public expectation and the enormous resources at the occupant's disposal have institutionalized presidential impact, not necessarily the greatness of the men who have occupied the office.[30]

Presidential scholar Fred Greenstein identifies several ways citizens make psychological use of the institutional presidency based upon his review of the literature and public opinion polls of the day. First, the office serves as a cognitive aid. The office provides citizens a vehicle for understanding government and its processes. At least, it provides a direct link to government. For children, it often provides the initial socialization into national citizenship. Second, the office provides an outlet for affect. The office reflects the mores and values of our nation. It speaks as to who we are, what we value, and what we hope to become. The office also serves as a means of vicarious participation. The president becomes a potential object of identification. Fourth, the office serves as a symbol of national unity. Finally, the office stands as a symbol of stability and predictability.[31]

In fact, Greenstein summarizes our relationship to the presidency with eight statements:

- The president is by far the best-known figure on the American political scene.
- The status of president is accorded great respect in American society.
- The president ordinarily is the first public official to come to the attention of young children.

- Even before they are substantively informed about the president's functions, children believe that he is exceptionally important—and that he is benign.
- Adult assessments of the performance of incumbent presidents fluctuate from time to time and differ from group to group, but in spite of this variation, adults normally have a favorable view of the president's performance.
- There is a significant tendency for citizens to rally to the support of the president, particularly when he acts in times of international crisis.
- Citizens seem to perceive and evaluate the president as a person, rather than in terms of his policy commitments or his skill in the specialized tasks of leadership.
- Finally, there is some scattered clinical evidence that, at least for a portion of the population, the president is the unconscious symbolic surrogate of childhood authority figures.[32]

In the early 1970s, presidential scholar James Barber argued that Americans look to their presidents to satisfy three sets of needs: the need for reassurance, a sense of progress, and a sense of legitimacy. He predicted that "people are hungry for a hero, one who fits the new age. . . . A good deal is riding on the question whether they will find a demagogue or a democrat as they search out a way to link their passions to their government."[33] Some have argued that Clinton represents the former, a "weather vane," guided by the ebb and flow of public opinion. How do we distinguish between a demagogue and a democrat? Does behavior inform us? Does character provide a clue?

PRESIDENTIAL CHARACTER

Presidential scholar Barbara Kellerman, in a recent analysis of presidential leadership, lamented that "of all the problems that beset leadership in America at the end of the twentieth century, the so-called character issue is perhaps the most troubling."[34] Just what is character? The term comes from the Greek word meaning "engraving." Character implies a deep, fixed, basic psychological structure. It is character that shapes an individual, and hence any occupant of the office.

For Renshon, character is "a consolidated psychological foundation that frames a person's responses to circumstances and is often responsible for the person's circumstances themselves."[35] While character may develop over time, the concept also implies limits. "Character, in its consolidated form, is not an ode to unlimited choice. It is a reflection of choices already made, of establishing emotional priorities, and of the methods one has developed to satisfy them."[36]

According to Len Marrella, president of the Center for Leadership and Ethics, "character is that which constitutes a person's true nature and being. A person of character seeks to discover and know the truth, decides what is right, and demonstrates the courage and commitment to act accordingly. Leaders of character can be trusted and this trust is the basis for effective cooperation. Effective professional relationships and successful effort to achieve organizational goals occur when there is trust."[37]

Character, to use Renshon's definition of basic identity, ideals, and values, becomes the basis for presidential judgment. Character provides the anchor, a framework through which a president sorts facts, evaluates evidence, and withstands outside pressures. "A president without a coherent personal or political identity, and the strong ideals and values that underlie it, is like a ship without a rudder. Subjected to strong currents, he runs the danger of drift, or worse."[38] For historian David McCullough, Truman epitomizes the notion of being grounded and comfortable with himself. "He knew who he was, he liked who he was. He liked Harry Truman. He enjoyed being Harry Truman. He was sounded, as is said. He stressed, 'I tried never to forget who I was, where I came from, and where I would go back to.'"[39]

Character is the core of a person's psychology and is the basic foundation upon which personality-structures develop and operate. As character shapes beliefs, it ultimately impacts style of behavior. Personal character and integrity provide the structure of our behavior. Character shapes our beliefs, attitudes, values, and thus ultimately our behavior. So character refers to one's underlying values, how they fare when tested. Character is more than a set of principles; it's in the execution of daily actions that reflect the principles or guidelines of daily life.

Is presidential character multidimensional or seamless? Because I argue that lying to the American people and under oath is unacceptable for any and all public leaders, character to me is indeed seamless. No matter how naïve to say, for me character, honor, truth, and public trust are not a matter of degrees. Behavior is either acceptable or unacceptable.

I strongly agree with Renshon that integrity is "an absolutely critical basis for evaluating the character and political performance of presidents."[40] The notion of integrity shapes and guides ambition and defines how we relate to others. The concept implies a sense of honesty. Integrity provides a basis for evaluating character. The notion of integrity shapes and guides ambition and defines how we relate to others. The word comes from "integer," meaning "whole." A person of integrity is whole in terms of character, values, and behavior.[41] Stephen Carter, the Yale jurist, argues that a moral person is one who has integrated various aspects of his life. Integration is manifest in one's ability to examine basic values, to publicly articulate those values, and to act consistently on them.[42] Renshon defines character integrity as "the consolidated capacity for fidelity to one's ideals even as one works to fulfill one's ambitions."[43]

Reagan speechwriter Peggy Noonan posits,

> [I]n a president, character is everything. A president doesn't have to be brilliant; Harry Truman wasn't brilliant, and he helped save Western Europe from Stalin. He doesn't have to be clever; you can hire clever. The White House is always full of quick-witted people with ready advice on how to flip a senator or implement a strategy. . . . You can't buy courage and decency, you can't rent a strong moral sense. A president must bring those things with him. If he does, they will give meaning and animation to the great practical requirement of the presidency: He must know why he's there and what he wants to do. *He has to have thought it through.* He needs to have, in that maligned word, but a good one nonetheless, a *vision* of the future he wishes to create. This is a function of thinking, of the mind, the brain.[44]

Presidential scholar Bruce Buchanan identifies three criteria of the cultural concept of character.[45] First is character itself. While character consists of many variables, among the most common are trustworthiness, personal demeanor, and mental and moral characteristics.

Second is integrity. A person with integrity is one who adheres to moral and ethical principles, who is of sound moral character. Integrity prevails in the presence of temptation, pressure, and tribulation. Think of the "historical" Washington. He was not known for his brilliance or intelligence, especially compared to such contemporaries as Alexander Hamilton or Thomas Jefferson. Washington was also not known as an eloquent speaker or as charismatic; actually, quite the opposite. However, historians respect his reserve, humility, dignity, personal authenticity, and unswerving dedication to democratic ideals despite great personal risk to life and property. In effect, Washington's moral reputation was a powerful political and personal resource. It was displayed at the end of the Revolutionary War by turning down twice the call to be "king."

Washington turned away from the temptations of personal ambition, voluntarily disbanded his army, and retired from public life.

Buchanan's final criterion is charisma, that quality that is difficult to quantify but easily recognized among great leaders. It is a composite of personal characteristics that evoke emotional allegiance. According to James Cannon, Gerald Ford, more than any other president of the twentieth century, was selected for his personal integrity and trustworthiness. "His peers in Congress put him in the White House because he told the truth and kept his word. . . . Gerald Ford was the right man in the right place at the right time to replace the President who had dishonored himself and the office. Ford personified what Nixon was not. Ford was honest. He could be trusted. Throughout twenty-five years in the House of Representatives, Ford had proved himself to be a man of integrity."[46]

The experience of remaining true to one's ideals, having done so under adversity, is fundamental to the development of character integrity. Thus, a president's integrity is confirmed by examining behavior, over time and through difficult circumstances, to see how the individual has handled personal and public dilemmas.[47]

CONCLUSION

How do we judge the character of candidates? Thomas Cronin and Michael Genovese offer several questions for consideration: Does the behavior in question exceed the boundaries of what most reasonable people would think of as acceptable in those circumstances? Is there a clear pattern of this behavior and not an isolated act or event? Does it affect job performance? While they concede that Clinton may be faulted on the first two questions, they doubt one could argue that his behavior impacted his job performance. In the following chapter, I will challenge their conclusion. Nevertheless, in the end, they claim the real test of presidential character may well be "does the president bring out the best in all of us?" and "does the president serve the best interests of the nation as a whole?"[48]

James McGregor Burns calls for "transforming leadership" that seeks "sustained and planned social transformation" and "raises the level of human conduct and ethical aspiration of both leader and led."[49] Such leadership responds to "fundamental human needs and American values."[50]

John Adams stated, a decade before our Declaration of Independence was written in Philadelphia in 1776, "Liberty cannot be preserved without general knowledge among the people who have the right to that knowledge and the desire to know. But besides this, they have a right, an indisputable, unalienable, indefeasible, divine right to that most dreaded and envied kind of knowledge—I mean of the character and conduct of their rulers."[51]

NOTES

1. Bruce Miroff, "The Contemporary Presidency: Moral Character in the White House: From Republican to Democratic," *Presidential Studies Quarterly*, 29, 1999, 708.
2. Miroff, "The Contemporary Presidency," 711.
3. Miroff, "The Contemporary Presidency," 711.
4. James Kouzes and Barry Posner, *Leadership Challenge*, 3rd edition (San Francisco: Jossey-Bass, 2002), 13.
5. Stephen Ambrose, "Dwight D. Eisenhower," in Character Above All, Robert A. Wilson, ed. (New York: Simon & Schuster, 1995), 61.
6. Clinton Rossiter, *The Federalist Papers* (New York: Mentor Books, 1961), 414.
7. Rossiter, *The Federalist Papers*, 455.
8. Rossiter, *The Federalist Papers*, 396.
9. Robert Wiebe, *The Opening of American Society* (New York: Vintage, 1984), 12.
10. Michael Genovese, *The Presidential Dilemma* (New York: HarperCollins, 1995), 107.
11. Genovese, *The Presidential Dilemma*, 89.
12. Kouzes and Posner, *Leadership Challenge*, 383.
13. Aristotle, *Nicomachean Ethics*, ib. 1102–3.
14. Richard Regan, *The Moral Dimensions of Politics* (New York: Oxford University Press, 1986), 14–18.
15. Rabindra Kanungo and Manuel Mendonca, *Ethical Dimensions of Leadership* (Thousand Oaks, CA: Sage, 1996).
16. Robert Dallek, "Can Clinton Still Govern?" *Washington Post National Weekly Edition*, October 5, 1998, 22
17. Robert Putnam, *Making Democracy Work: Civic Traditions in Modern Italy* (Princeton, NJ: Princeton University Press, 1993).
18. Putnam, *Making Democracy Work*, 10.
19. Kouzes and Posner, *Leadership Challenge*, 24–25.
20. Dennis Thompson, *Political Ethics and Public Office* (Cambridge, MA: Harvard University Press, 1987), 83.
21. Marvin Olasky, *The American Leadership Tradition* (New York: Free Press, 1999), 7.
22. Thompson, *Political Ethics and Public Office*, 127.
23. Mike Huckabee, *Character Is the Issue* (Nashville, TN: Broadman & Holman, 1997), 57.

24. Kouzes and Posner, *Leadership Challenge*, 394.
25. Olasky, *The American Leadership Tradition*, 89.
26. Olasky, *The American Leadership Tradition*, 267.
27. William Hitt, *Ethics and Leadership* (Columbus, OH: Battelle Press, 1990), 3–4.
28. Kouzes and Posner, *Leadership Challenge*, 28.
29. Bruce Buchanan, *The Citizen's Presidency* (Washington, DC: Congressional Quarterly, 1987), 1–15.
30. Stanley A. Renshon, *High Hopes: The Clinton Presidency and the Politics of Ambition* (New York: New York University Press, 1996), 4–5.
31. Fred Greenstein, "Popular Images of the President," in *Perspectives on the Presidency*, Stanley Bach and George Sulzner, eds. (Lexington, MA: D. C. Heath, 1974), 134–43.
32. Greenstein, "Popular Images of the President," 136–39.
33. James D. Barber, "The Presidency: What Americans Want," in *Perspectives on the Presidency*, Stanley Bach and George Sulzner, eds. (Lexington, MA: D. C. Heath, 1974), 145–49, 151.
34. Barbara Kellerman, *Reinventing Leadership* (Albany: State University of New York Press, 1999), 213.
35. Renshon, *High Hopes*, 37.
36. Renshon, *High Hopes*, 37.
37. Len Marrella, *In Search of Ethics* (Sanford, FL: DC Press, 2001), 182.
38. Marrella, *In Search of Ethics*, 251.
39. David McCullough, "Harry S. Truman," in *Character Above All*, Robert A. Wilson, ed. (New York: Simon & Schuster, 1995), 40.
40. Renshon, *High Hopes*, 40.
41. William J. Bennett, *The Death of Outrage* (New York: Free Press, 1998), 37.
42. Stephen Carter, *Integrity* (New York: HarperCollins, 1996), 8–19.
43. Renshon, *High Hopes*, 41.
44. Peggy Noonan, "Ronald Reagan," in *Character Above All*, Robert A. Wilson, ed. (New York: Simon & Schuster, 1995), 202–45.
45. Buchanan, *The Citizen's Presidency*, 32–40.
46. James Cannon, "Gerald R. Ford," in *Character Above All*, Robert A. Wilson, ed. (New York: Simon & Schuster, 1995), 146.
47. Renshon, *High Hopes*, 43.
48. Thomas Cronin and Michael Genovese, "President Clinton and Character Questions," *Presidential Studies Quarterly*, 28 (4), 892. Accessed online using InfoTrac library services.
49. James McGregor Burns, *The Power to Lead* (New York: Simon & Schuster, 1984), 20.
50. Burns, *The Power to Lead*, 16.
51. As quoted in McCullough, "Harry S. Truman," 59.

5

The Case of William Jefferson Clinton

Telling the truth slowly.

—MICHAEL McCURRY, press secretary in
the Clinton administration

Historically, there has always been some concern about the power, legitimacy, and effectiveness of the presidency. Especially since about 1965, historians and political scientists have questioned the viability of the office. Some argued that real concerns had their origins in the United States' intervention in a civil war in Indochina. Our "modest" intervention grew, in a span of a few years, from a minor distraction in American foreign policy into an engulfing national obsession. Meanwhile, domestically the nation was bombarded by the "crises" of inflation, race, pollution, crime, drugs, energy, and world food shortages. The "crisis" reached its peak with the resignation of a president of the United States. Watergate and Nixon's subsequent forced resignation sparked reflection, by many Americans, on the office of president. Many Americans realized for the first time that "the checks were not checking" and "the balances were not balancing." More specifically, there were concerns of governmental secrecy, war-making authority without congressional or public consultation, extensive use of executive privilege, and wholesale violation of personal rights with unregulated wiretapping, enemy lists, and abuse of the judicial process.

Without precedent, in the Watergate crisis, the president and his aides stood accused of violation of constitutional liberties, commitment of criminal acts, and various other behaviors incompatible with recognized democratic processes. The "imperial presidency" became the academic catchword for the process of presidential aggrandizement and institutionalization that began under Franklin D. Roosevelt. Some observers believe the office has become unmanageable.

Because the presidency is more than a managerial office, any serious consideration of the potential of the office must recognize the public's perceptions, attitudes, and beliefs about the nature of the office. Institutional structures are only a small part of the presidency. As argued in the third chapter, the office exists in a cultural context consisting of specific norms and expectations.

Some would argue that the nation's mythic, symbolic expectations of the office are no longer apropos to meet the challenges or realities of the twenty-first century. I certainly hope this is not the case. If so, we have lost a very unique feature of the institution and our history. Virtually all contemporary presidential scholars praise the devaluation of the "heroic presidency."

For example, Shawn and Trevor Parry-Giles actually like the notion that as images of presidents proliferate, we are more likely to be skeptical of what presidents proclaim and advocate, thus further eroding presidential powers they think have expanded "far beyond their constitutional parameters." "The overextended idolatry commonly invested in the presidency and individual presidents may lessen, thus investing in the public a greater responsibility for the success of the U.S. democratic experiment."[1]

Bruce Miroff concurs with the Perry-Gileses with the notion that the decline of presidential image and even power is a welcomed development. "It has not been healthy for a democratic society to become so dependent on the leadership of a single individual. A democracy needs active citizens, not passive spectators to presidential heroics."[2] However, an important part of my argument is that even with the decline, we have not witnessed increased voter turnout or citizen participation or knowledge. If anything, public cynicism about politics and politicians has increased.

At this rate, how long will it be until Old Glory loses its meaning and power as a symbol of our heritage, the values of the nation, and the very fabric for which millions of citizens paid the ultimate price?

THE CASE OF WILLIAM JEFFERSON CLINTON

During the impeachment considerations, it was the job of Congress to consider the legal, partisan, and constitutional issues. However, it was up to the American people to determine presidential legitimacy. By this I mean whether the president acted in such a way to bring shame and harm to the office. Did his behavior impair his ability to perform his legal, constitutional, and social role? I think so. And I think Bill Clinton should have resigned.

There is no question that ultimate impeachment and Congressional removal from office alters the verdict of the people by way of the presidential election of 1996. Thus, honor suggests self-removal. At least Richard Nixon resigned. Perhaps too late, but he did understand the nature of his harm to the office, to the integrity of democratic government, and to the American people. Bill Clinton showed no such regard.

Bill Bennett, a partisan and certainly no fan of Clinton, does make an interesting point that by Senator Gary Hart's withdrawal from the 1988 presidential race because of the sexual scandal with Donna Rice, he actually *affirmed* public standards of public behavior. In the end, he showed regret and offered an apology: "Through thoughtlessness and misjudgment I've let each of you down. And I deeply regret that."[3]

Marvin Olasky raises the same point: "It is much easier to crusade about international justice than to practice justice in our homes and offices. It is much easier for a man to orate about protecting the rights of women than to protect one woman next to him. But if President Clinton were to show that respect for the presidency required confession and resignation, and that raising the bar in that fashion was more important than personal comfort, he would be handing his successors a presidency diminished by many of his actions but augmented by his last one."[4]

A single individual action or behavior may indeed be viewed as an unfortunate lapse. However, a series of such behaviors, misstatements, and public lies constitutes a massive moral collapse. In the case of Clinton, with each denial came a new revelation. Public deceit upon deceit constitutes the absence of respect for the office and the general public. Diminished moral authority has its own implications and consequences. With each official pronouncement, motives are questioned. Words are parsed in a search for meaning and truth. Remember those who claim that Clinton's international response of bombing Saddam Hussein was merely a diversion from the headlines at home, the so-called "wag the dog" effect? His actions kept us in turmoil for months and months while he knew the truth, a truth not kept in silence, but released slowly through frequent denial, distortion, and misstatements.

Late in the impeachment scandal, Clinton's close personal friend, White House staff member, and longtime political operative George Stephanopoulos asked what most Americans pondered: "How could a president so intelligent, so compassionate, so public-spirited, and so conscious of his place in history act in such a stupid, selfish, and self-destructive manner?"[5] He reveals, "As I wrote and rewrote, I came to see how Clinton's shamelessness is a key to his political success."[6] The scandal, from Bennett's perspective, demonstrated "the worst elements of Bill Clinton's private *and* public character; reckless and irresponsible private behavior; habitual lying; abuse of power."[7] By Stanley Renshon's analysis, Clinton is a president of extremes combining immense personal and political skills with equally evident personal and political flaws.[8]

During the 1992 presidential campaign, Clinton proclaimed that the election would be a test of not just his character, but that of the American people. Indeed, how prophetic. The Clinton presidency provided several challenges. As Robert Shogan observes, "For Clinton, the test was whether his inherent gifts for leadership would outweigh the darker impulses of his nature. For the country, the issue was what standards of personal behavior Americans would accept from their president. And for the system, the challenge was whether it could respond responsibly to the tensions created by the controversies over Clinton's character."[9]

J. T. Young thinks Clinton "has reduced (for better or worse) the dominant role that the presidency has played since 1933." In effect, "no president in modern history of the United States has so willingly and so thoroughly reduced—diminished—the role of his office as has Clinton."[10]

Political scientist Martha Kumar argues that the personality of presidents impacts the institution. "The personal style of a president permeates every corner and every crevice in the building and influences the actions of every individual. Staff members take their cues from him both in the priorities they establish and the messages they send out."[11]

Longtime Clinton observer and writer for the *Arkansas Democrat-Gazette* Paul Greenberg characterizes the "Clintonized culture of America in the 90's" as "a remarkably spiritless spirit: full of sentimentality without emotion, leadership without direction, idealism without sacrifice, policy without decisions, great ambition without clear purpose, unending talk without much meaning or action . . . and a degree of self-absorption remarkable for even American society, which always seems to be taking its own temperature."[12]

Presidential Lies

At the heart of the controversy with Bill Clinton is simply the issue of lying. Private lies become public lies. My problem is not about "private" sex but his public lying to me on the matter. As president, in the

Roosevelt Room of the White House, behind the official podium with the presidential seal, looking straight into the cameras, wagging his finger *at me*, he emphatically declared, "Listen to me. I did not have sexual relations with that woman, Monica Lewinsky. I never told anybody to lie, not a single time, never. These allegations are false." We would see this statement over and over again, for weeks that turned into months. We know now, of course, based on twenty hours of taped conversations, thirty-seven visits to the White House by Lewinsky (nine sexual encounters, phone sex between fourteen and sixteen times[13]), Betty Currie's testimony, the infamous blue dress, a brooch, a hat pin, and much other collaborating evidence, that Clinton's statement was anything but true.

On August 17, 1998, in the Map Room of the White House, Clinton read a statement to the grand jury. "When I was alone with Ms. Lewinsky on certain occasions in early 1996 and once in early 1997, I engaged in conduct that was wrong. These encounters did not consist of sexual intercourse; they did not constitute sexual relations as I understood that term to be defined at my January 17, 1998 deposition. But they did involve inappropriate intimate contact. These inappropriate encounters ended at my insistence in early 1997. I also had occasional telephone conversations with Ms. Lewinsky that included inappropriate sexual banter. I regret that what began as a friendship came to include this conduct, and I take full responsibility for my actions."[14]

We further learn that fateful day that Clinton did indeed have sex with Gennifer Flowers, a fact he denied as "vicious lies" during the 1992 presidential campaign. In January, he said he did not recall being alone with Lewinsky; now he admitted to being alone with her fourteen times, just three weeks before his Paula Jones testimony. That same evening, at 10 p.m., in the Map Room, Clinton addressed the nation. He provided a four-and-a-half-minute, 543-word statement. He confessed that his public comments gave "a false impression" and that he "misled people, including even my wife. I deeply regret that."[15]

However, the statement and drama were classic Clinton in so many ways. We learned to parse his words, for they always seem to raise more questions than provide answers. Was his finger-wagging denial a lie or a "false impression"? Was he "legally accurate" to exclude oral sex from the explicit definition of sexual relations? Or when he could not recall being alone with Lewinsky? He claims he never asked anyone to lie, but acknowledged providing leading and prompting questions to Betty Currie. The simple fact is, in the words of James Bovard, "Clinton was a master of the big lie."[16]

In late 1997 and early in 1998, Clinton could have told the truth about his relationship with Monica Lewinsky, confessed his sin, and trusted the American people to accept the confession and offer forgiveness. However, "because he was unwilling to confess that he is a sinner stuck in a rut, he apparently was willing to perjure himself, tamper with witnesses, and suppress evidence."[17]

The legal consequences of his lying are clear. He settled the Paula Jones case and was found in contempt of court with "clear and convincing evidence" of "false, misleading, and evasive answers that were designed to obstruct the judicial process" in the Jones deposition. On the last day in office, Clinton finally entered into a plea bargain to avoid criminal prosecution for knowingly providing false testimony under oath. As part of the plea bargain, Clinton had to accept a five-year suspension of his license to practice law in Arkansas and pay legal fees of $25,000.[18] Clinton did not even appeal when a federal court held him in contempt. This from someone who was trained in the law and upon numerous occasions as a public servant swore to faithfully execute the office and to "preserve, protect, and defend the Constitution of the United States."

The irony is beyond me. At the height of the impeachment process, a *Washington Post* poll revealed that 65 percent of those polled approved the way Clinton was handling the presidency while only 35 percent thought he was honest and trustworthy. Just 29 percent of the group thought he had high personal morals and ethical standards.[19] Even more telling, an ABC poll in December 1998 found that 86 percent of Americans believed Clinton indeed lied under oath and that 63 percent believed he had obstructed justice. Yet 60 percent did not want him to be removed from office.[20] However, according to a *Washington Post* poll of March 1998, 37 percent of Americans favored resignation, 22 percent a formal reprimand, 21 percent an apology, and 16 percent no action. Thus, 59 percent favored some form of action against Clinton for his behavior.[21]

According to U.S. Code, Title 18, Section 1503, such corruption can be punished by imprisonment for up to ten years plus a fine.[22] At the time of the plea bargain, three federal judges had been impeached and convicted of perjury. In fact, more than one hundred persons were serving time in federal prison for the crime, a felony.[23]

David Schippers, the majority counsel of the House Judiciary Committee, succinctly stated the politically obvious during the impeachment hearings: "The President, then, has lied under oath in a civil deposition, lied under oath in a criminal grand jury. He lied to the people, he lied to his cabinet, he lied to his top aides, and now he's lied under oath to the Congress of the United States. There's no one left to lie to."[24]

Lying to the American people is a clear betrayal of trust. President Clinton lied repeatedly, openly, and directly to the American people. Is it "OK" to lie in judicial proceedings? Can we trust our system of justice if people do not feel obligated to tell the truth under oath? Should the president ever be "above the law"? Consider the simple fact that Ronald Blackley, chief of staff to former agriculture secretary Mike Espy, was sentenced to twenty-seven months in prison by federal judge Royce Lamberth for making false statements under oath.[25]

There is no question that President Clinton has shown a willingness to distort, at least shade meaning, at the most outright lie. From a national perspective, we saw this pattern during the 1992 presidential campaign with evasive answers to questions concerning his marriage, the draft, Gennifer Flowers, and his use of marijuana. We saw it during his first term in Whitewater, "travelgate," and "filegate," to name a few. Then we saw it during 1996 questioning surrounding fund-raising. Then, finally, we saw it in the questions on Lewinsky, depositions, impeachment, and the last-minute pardons.

Carl Cannon, White House correspondent for the *Baltimore Sun*, observed in 1995, "This president salts his remarks with so many inventions, half-truths, and self-serving exaggerations that reporters who cover him often have to choose between truth-squadding every speech or ignoring his fibs."[26]

Presidential scholars Colin Campbell and Bert Rockman recognize that "Clinton did manage to demonstrate without much doubt that his word was worthless, that lying came easy to him, and that his behavior and lack of self-control toward women left him a perpetual adolescent."[27] Robert Patterson, military aide to the president, was simply amazed at how routine lying was with Clinton. Even in inconsequential golf games, he would cheat with ball placements and extra shots. Patterson recounts a time when he kept the actual score and, at the end of the course, compared the president's scorecard with the actual score. Even talking to the press, Clinton claimed he shot a 79. Actually, it was 92.[28]

Rich Lowry concludes, "A variety of deceptive machinations were ready at hand: the advice to Monica to file a false affidavit, the coaching of his secretary, Betty Currie, the lying to his intimates and the public. None of these tactics was novel to Clinton, nor did he evince the least hesitation in resorting to them. They were second nature, part of the grease that had fueled his political rise."[29]

In terms of honesty, how does Clinton rate? Presidential scholar Renshon puts it this way. "If by honesty one means that Clinton almost always says what he knows to be true and almost always doesn't say what he knows to be untrue, that he is substantially candid about all the implications of his policies and not just their advantages, then the preponderance of evidence points in one direction. Judged by these standards, Clinton has not been honest with the public, and his behavior to date does not give confidence in his trustworthiness."[30] Because of an "idealized" view of himself, Clinton seems unaware of the discrepancies between what he says and what he does. "Whether this comes from the sense of not wanting to be limited in any way personally or politically (itself a possible manifestation of grandiosity), or whether it comes from a sense of being special and therefore entitled to operate differently, or both, is not yet clear." In effect, Clinton always wants everything both ways.[31]

Character

There is a growing plethora of books attempting to address the psyche and various facets of Clinton's personality, leadership, style and character. As is the case with most presidents, Clinton is complex. Bruce Miroff sees two rather clear and distinct aspects of Clinton. "The 'appealing' Clinton is exceptionally bright, energetic, optimistic, charming, and caring. The 'appalling' Clinton is exceptionally cunning, manipulative, evasive, petulant, and self-indulgent."[32] However, for presidential scholar Bert Rockman, "whatever his intelligence and perhaps desire to do public good and whatever his political acumen, Clinton's personal and perhaps even public life is scarred. His character is deeply flawed."[33] Rich Lowry sums up Clinton and his presidential leadership this way: "Ultimately, the ingredients of presidential leadership aren't complicated: It takes a clean set of principles and character, Clinton had neither."[34]

Renshon argues there are three core elements to Bill Clinton's character. First is his substantial level of ambition. Second is his immense self-confidence, coupled with an idealized view of his fidelity to the ideals he espouses. Finally, there is a distinct and powerful turn toward others in his interpersonal relationships, motivated by his strong need for validation of his idealized view of himself.[35]

In a broader perspective, Clinton lacks "character integrity" or the ability to maintain boundaries and consistencies among the things he says and his actions. Renshon finds Clinton's style of presidential leadership "episodic, discontinuous," "intensely personal and political," and "ideologically ambiguous."[36]

One result of Clinton's idealized vision of himself is that he never makes mistakes. Consequently, Clinton never accepts responsibility for his actions. He is always a victim. Thus, Clinton finds it difficult to be contrite because of his "inability to engage in self-examination and his propensity to believe only the best about himself, his motives, his intent, his desires. For Clinton," according to presidential scholar Stephen Wayne, "being caught is being victimized, the object of a political witch-hunt by his enemies."[37] Even in discussing his last-minute pardons, Clinton claimed being "mugged one more time on the way out the door." Louis Fisher concludes, "He did not reflect on how much his personal judgments and misjudgments contributed to—and deserved—the criticism that came his way."[38]

Renshon suggested three resulting dilemmas of the Clinton presidency in terms of political leadership.[39] First, there is in Clinton "a willingness to shade meaning and be less than forthright." It didn't take the Lewinsky affair to learn of such tendency. During his campaign in 1992 there was evidence based upon his evasive answers regarding the draft, Gennifer Flowers, and marijuana use. Second, he noted "we can also see these nuances in this administration's very strong concern with appearances." The Clinton administration went to great lengths to portray a close, loving marriage relationship. He could turn on emotion at the drop of a hat, or more precisely, the presence of a camera. In the words of Lowry, "Clinton was the new, sensitive man elevated to high office: sentimental and easily moved to tears, undisciplined and self-indulgent, endlessly and thoughtlessly expressive, schooled in the language and attitudes of therapy. . . . He was a soft man for soft age."[40] Finally, which is perhaps just the nature of contemporary politics, "there also appears to be a tendency to claim more for the results of Clinton's policies than are warranted."[41]

On the eve of Bill Clinton's electoral victory in 1992, the editorial in the *Arkansas Democrat-Gazette* provided a forecast of the pending Clinton years.

> As for who Bill Clinton might be, what he stands for, what principles and policies he represents . . . none of that is as clear as his political pizzazz. . . . Bill Clinton is a master politician, but what principles, if any inform his politics? He embodies the glossy spirit of the times, but is it a spirit to be encouraged? Are there any steadfast principles—besides winning the next election—that he would never compromise to win popularity? Who knows? And if we don't, how can we recommend him to America as a leader? . . . Finally and sadly, there is the unavoidable subject of character in a presidential candidate. Surely even his supporters, or at least those not entirely blinded by the Clinton glitz, can see that—whatever one thinks of young Clinton's adventures

with the draft and antiwar demonstrations—he regularly dissembled about both over the course of some twenty years. Nor would they deny that he broke his enthusiastic promise not to run for president this year but to stay on and discharge the duties of governor, as he solemnly swore to do. But it is not the duplicitousness in his politics that concerns so much as the polished ease, the almost habitual, casual, articulate way he bobs and weaves.[42]

Clinton observer and journalist Paul Greenberg notes, "Politicians aren't given nicknames, they earn them." Slick Willie first appeared in an editorial in the *Arkansas-Democrat Gazette* on September 27, 1980.[43] Greenberg writes, "Credit for the popularity of Slick Willie as shorthand for the political persona of Bill Clinton must go chiefly to Bill Clinton himself; he vindicated that title through years of diligent effort. To claim that his vacuous zigs and zags are really only a cover for liberalism, or for any other coherent political philosophy, is to miss the central theme of his career, and to overlook what is most vulnerable about his appeal this year."

Like everything else related to the Clinton presidency, the "character issue" became an object for strategic study. Clinton pollster Stanley Greenberg predicted that the "character issue" would only become an issue if Clinton did not produce, or move the country forward. In effect, "Clinton was in a race against himself. If the productive Clinton could stay ahead of the Clinton about whom people had questions, he would be successful."[44]

What has Clinton said about his own character? First, he conceptualizes character as "a journey, not a destination," not about concrete values or actions, but a lifelong passage, always "in process." Thus, for Clinton, character is not static, set, or frozen. In effect, his character lapses or mistakes are "normal," "human," and events from which to learn life lessons. From this perspective, his character is still and ever evolving.[45] In 1992, Bill Clinton is quoted as saying, "I don't have any reservations about the strength of my character."[46]

Renshon observes that "in spite of being in elected public life since 1976 and having dealt with domestic policy for over twenty-five years before assuming the presidency, Clinton seems not to have developed a real synthesis and integration of the ideals, values, and principles that would make it possible to proceed on other than a case-by-case basis."[47]

Clinton also avoids yes or no responses, drawing clear lines, and making hard choices that are a routine part of every presidential responsibility. The reason for this tendency, according to Renshon, is that making clear-cut decisions runs counter to his ambitions and his idealized view of himself.

"For Clinton, making choices means accepting limits, which is extraordinarily difficult for a person with such substantial ambitions and a high level of self-confidence in his ability to accomplish his irreconcilable purposes."[48]

Longtime observer Greenberg concurs, noting, "He has mastered the art of equivocation. There is something almost inhuman in his smoother responses that send a shiver up the spine. It is not the compromises he has made that trouble so much as the unavoidable suspicion that he has no great principles to compromise."[49]

After Clinton was in office a little more than a year, journalist Elizabeth Drew concluded that "the public remained hesitant about him, and, if anything, had grown increasingly so. The cluster of defects that could be listed under the term 'character'—his 'Slick Willie' aspect and all that that conveyed, his inclination to avoid responsibility for some of his acts, his lack of discipline, and his reckless streak (at lease in the past)—endangered his presidency."[50]

In terms of Clinton's political leadership, Renshon asserts there is a "willingness to shade meaning and be less than forthright," a "very strong concern with appearances," and "a tendency to claim more for the results" of policies than is warranted.[51]

Bob Woodward assesses Clinton this way: "People feel, and I think rightly, that they're not being leveled with. . . . There is this tendency in Clinton which you see all through his life of, 'How do we spin our way out of it? How do we put out 10 percent of the truth? How do we try to conceal or delay or obfuscate?' And that is a profound problem."[52]

Back in 1994, Joe Klein wrote in *Newsweek* magazine, "A clear pattern has emerged—of delay, of obfuscation, of lawyering the truth. The litany of offenses is as familiar as it is depressing. . . . With the Clintons, the story always is subject to further revision. The misstatements are always incremental. The 'misunderstandings' are always innocent—casual, irregular: promiscuous. Trust is squandered in dribs and drabs. Does this sort of behavior also infect the president's public life, his formulation of policy? Clearly, it does."[53]

Perhaps much of the sense of personal waffling, the lack of principles and consistency leading to a lack of basic trust, was due to the extensive use of public opinion polling by the Clinton administration. According to Howard Kurtz, for this presidency, opinion polls were "virtually a religion."[54] Of course all presidents are concerned with public opinion. Presidents since Richard Nixon have actively incorporated polling as part of their decision-making process. Between 1968 and 1988, polling was used primarily for speech writing and designing political strategies.[55]

However, for the Clinton White House, continuous surveying of public opinion, especially in the second term, became a tool for political survival. Previous administrations would review monthly poll numbers. However, the Clinton administration would receive weekly and even sometimes daily polling data. Clinton used poll data to provide clear policy and strategic prescriptions and actions.[56] "It was not only that Clinton spent far more time, money, and energy on tracking opinion polls than previous presidents," according to Graham Wilson, "but that specialists in public opinion and campaigning such as Morris were much more involved in policymaking than in the past, and policy initiatives were more thoroughly pre-tested on the public."[57]

Even Clinton's use of polls became an ethical issue during the impeachment hearings. His decision to poll on the subject of perjury, obstruction of justice, and sex in order to develop a public strategy for political survival was called into question. Pollster Dick Morris discovered that the public would forgive adultery, even telling Monica Lewinsky to lie to cover up the affair. However, the public would be less likely to forgive subornation of perjury. Through polling, operatives developed the strategy of separating the private misconduct from "professional" acts as president. The ethical dilemma is presidential use of polling to develop a public relations strategy in order to excuse an illegal act.[58] In the words of Diane Heith, "where is the line between inviting the public into the political process via the polling apparatus and manipulating or misusing the public for personal rather than public good?"[59]

Clinton's pattern of behavior is directly illustrated by a quick review of the strategies and tactics of crisis communication during the Lewinsky scandal. An essential part of the strategy was the use of surrogates to frame the debate and to define or redefine the actions and/or behaviors of the president. Of course, the use of surrogates by elected officials is not new. What was unique about the Clinton White House was the composition of surrogates (from Hillary to staffers to legislators) and the pattern of response: issue a direct denial, attack opposition/identify scapegoat, send out surrogates with scripted verbatim responses, and then go to the heartland. By Renshon's analysis, "President Clinton and his advocates used every means possible to raise questions about the evidence; attack the credibility of his accusers; deny that he had done anything legally wrong; and portray himself, at worst, as someone who had perhaps suffered from a lapse of judgment but not of lawful behavior—while seeking the public's understanding for his 'all too human' failings."[60] Miroff characterizes Clinton's conduct in the entire Lewinsky scandal as being marked by the lack of self-control, the absence of honor, and the exhibition of shamelessness.[61]

There were four rather distinct phases to the then evolving Lewinsky crisis: news story breaks, public denial, deposition/admission, and then the impeachment hearings. The Clinton presidency found itself in what I characterize as a rhetorical triangle (see figure). At the heart of the rhetorical triangle is public opinion. Each point of the rhetorical triangle represents a group of responses or arguments intended to direct, redirect, or strengthen public opinion. One point of the triangle represents traditional political concerns of the presidency. This includes general considerations of political leadership. For Clinton, it includes such concerns as his place in history and his moral authority, and more pragmatic concerns of maintaining political viability among core constituent groups and the then pending 1998 midterm elections. Another end of the triangle represents policy considerations

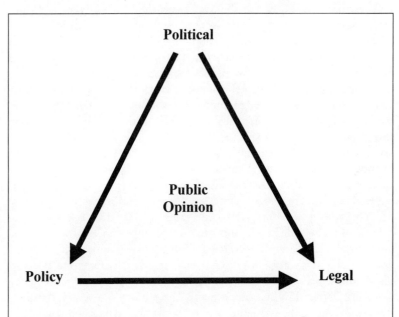

Political Arguments: aspects of political leadership, place in history, moral authority, impact upon elections, etc.

Policy Arguments: legislative agenda, past legislative accomplishments, future legislative initiatives, etc.

Legal Arguments: litigation (criminal and civil), legal allegations, impeachment proceedings, etc.

Clinton Scandal "Rhetorical Triangle"

revealed in the administration's legislative agenda and specific issue initiatives in education, health care, the economy, and so forth. In effect, policy arguments reflect his legislative resume with past accomplishments and future initiatives. Finally, the third area represents legal concerns to include current and future litigation (criminal and civil), legal allegations, and impeachment considerations.

When public opinion and hence public discussion dominated in one area, the White House attempted to shift or move the public discussion and hence public opinion to another area of the triangle, not unlike the movement of the control panel on a Ouija Board. However, there was a clear pattern or flow of argument of White House response. For example, when political concerns of the presidency dominated public discussion and opinion (i.e., leadership capacity, moral authority, etc.), White House surrogates attempted to shift the discussion and attention to policy matters or legislative initiatives and efforts of the president. However, when policy discussions become evaluative and presidential effectiveness questioned, White House surrogates focused on more legal arguments (i.e., current poll numbers, general public support of the president, presidential contrition, the idea that behavior is not an impeachable offense, etc.) to maintain public support for the president. Ultimately, a focus on and discussion of legal concerns led to more political considerations of presidential leadership, moral authority, and potential impact upon future Democratic Party electoral challenges. Thus, the pattern of public discussion and White House response moved from legal considerations to political considerations to policy considerations and so on.

The administration had a wide range of individuals speaking in defense of the president. The sheer number of appearances of some of the individuals is staggering. Of course, the frequency of appearances reflects not only the persistent effort to get their side of the story out, but also the need to have some "voice" on all the various cable shows and outlets, especially CNN, MSNBC, and so forth. The primary surrogates were Paul Begala, Robert Bennett, James Carville, Lanny Davis, Rahm Emanuel, and Dick Morris. Early in the crisis, Robert Bennett, Erskine Bowles, and David Kendall were active in providing statements. The primary defenders were Paul Begala, Lanny Davis, and Rahm Emanuel. James Carville, of course, was an "unofficial" surrogate of the White House.

The list of strategies and tactics are equally wide ranging. Richard Pious notes that the Lewinsky scandal cover-up followed prior patterns: "Clinton mortgaged himself to those involved in his affairs, and he paid interest to have his secrets kept"; Clinton responds to scandal by using

"debasing language, offering plausible denials, and circling the wagons."
When all else fails, he moves "from arguing the facts to arguing ad homi-
nen or tu quoque (i.e., you're just as bad)." In sum, "he denied an affair
with Lewinsky but initially claimed the relationship was complex and later
that it was inappropriate, and promised that he would eventually provide
a complete explanation—at least until his acquittal, after which the White
House indicated that no explanation would be forthcoming."[62]

There is certainly a pattern of conduct throughout Clinton's life,
whether it's in the Monica Lewinsky, Paula Jones, and Kathleen Willey
episodes or the much older college ROTC incident. It is simply the use of
public office ultimately for private ends and gratification. Greenberg wrote
in an editorial in August of 1992 that "then and now, Bill Clinton's chief
political principle has been his own political advancement. Moderate or
liberal, in Arkansas or out, trickle-down conservative or populist orator,
young or less young, he has never deviated from that single, obsessive goal.
Such ambition saves a fellow from being a liberal—or anything else."[63]

Private versus Public Behavior

As already mentioned, I was surprised by the public's acceptance of the
distinction between public and private behaviors of leaders. It was interesting to hear the range of reactions to the relationship of personal behaviors and the conduct of public business. Some responses were just
"political," along the lines of "Clinton is a Democrat, I don't like
Republicans, and to make matters worse, Ken Starr is conducting a witch
hunt." Others took a more pragmatic perspective. For example, some
expressed something like, "I don't like Clinton's behavior, but I like his
policies and the economy is going well." Then there were the responses
of "What's the big deal? We knew he was 'Slick Willie' when we elected
him." Finally, there were those who really think that the private life has
no bearing on public accomplishments.

There are several reasons why the public could accept this distinction.
First, for years we have been learning more and more about past presidential
faults, peccadilloes, and problems ranging from Thomas Jefferson's alleged
affair with Sally Hemings to the one-night stands of John F. Kennedy.
However, the so-called "everyone's doing it" defense is very cynical. As adults,
when confronted with such rationale from our children, we ask, "If everyone
was jumping off the bridge, does that make it wise for you to do so?"

Second, Americans believe that members of the press are becoming too
obtrusive, going too far in their investigations of public officials. They became

sympathetic to cries for zones of privacy by celebrities and public personali-
ties. The constant intrusions became too frequent and too revealing.

Third, Americans during the 1990s were redefining morality. Social
relativism became the norm. Social judgment became virtually nonexist-
ent. Tolerance, of anything and everything, became a prized virtue.

Finally, as the president mirrors us as "average citizens" rather than
serve as a role model, our expectations were lowered for the occupant of
the office. The Clinton scandals desensitized us to presidential scandals,
especially involving sex. As doubt about the integrity of politicians grew,
we became less shocked by their behaviors. Thus, the decline in expectations of public leaders was reinforced, nearly on a weekly basis, by the
Clinton administration as the "incidents" mounted. As a result, we
adopted a "Machiavellian idea of political virtue, where morality is irrelevant to the achievement of political results."[64]

The public, of course, thought that Clinton's deceptions were
attempts to cover up a private scandal, not a public one. Some pundits
even claimed that his misdeeds in no way impacted his ability to lead the
country, to perform his constitutional duties. I disagree. It had consequences for him, for the nation, and for the system.

Clinton never really engendered the trust and respect of the majority of citizens as Reagan did and other successful presidents do. He
became a very polarizing president, never winning a popular majority of
votes in two elections. As a result of his personal reputation, Clinton was
severely limited on the range of issues he could address that hinged on
questions of values, personal accountability, and responsibility.

First, there was more at stake than his personal reputation. The lies
he told about sex were told not only to the American people in the role
as president, but also under oath as part of a criminal investigation. There
was damage done to the public's attitudes and trust toward political institutions. We witnessed a rise in cynicism and lower voter turnout.

In addition, there are political and policy implications. There were
the constant distractions and time spent plotting legal strategies rather
than pursuing policy goals. In fact, there were weeks when Clinton could
not leave the White House in order to avoid answering questions from
members of the press. He was restricted to televised speeches before
highly controlled and selected audiences. On one occasion, Clinton dis-
patched his secretaries of state and defense and his national security advisor to a CNN-staged event at Ohio State University. He dared not go
personally and have to answer questions about sex. The scandal kept
Clinton from pushing an aggressive free-trade agenda, from bombing al

Qaeda targets, from properly confronting Saddam Hussein,[65] and largely from getting Al Gore elected president.

There were institutional consequences to his behavior. In response to the Paula Jones sexual harassment lawsuit, Clinton's attorneys had to appeal to the Supreme Court to reverse a lower-court ruling attempting to grant him immunity to such suits as long as he served as president. It was only the third time in history the Supreme Court had ruled on a fundamental conflict over constitutional authority. The other times were in 1952, when the Supreme Court held that Truman had exceeded his powers when he seized control of the steel industry to end a strike, and in 1974, when the court ordered President Nixon to hand over White House tape recordings to the Watergate prosecutor.[66]

Presidential scholars Colin Campbell and Bert Rockman think "future presidents will step into an office that by legal precedent is now a weaker one than Clinton came to. Clinton bears much of the responsibility for its weakening; so do Kenneth Starr and the Paula Jones attorneys. Ultimately, of course, the judicial branch has opened up a can of worms by ruling on matters over which it has limited competency and, strictly speaking, jurisdiction."[67]

What was missing from the Clinton presidency is the moral authority that usually accompanies the office. His election, despite the wide range of indiscretions and indulgences, provided several dilemmas related to sexual mores. For example, General Joseph Ralston of the Air Force had to withdraw his name as a candidate for chairman of the Joint Chiefs of Staff because he had previously been involved in an extramarital affair. First Lieutenant Kelly Flinn, one of the few female fighter pilots, had to resign from service because of an active-duty adulterous relationship. In addition, the army's top enlisted man, Sergeant Major Gene McKinney, was charged with sexual harassment. In all these cases, during which time Clinton was using the courts to delay Paula Jones's sexual harassment lawsuit, just what could Clinton as leader, as commander in chief, say? To perform well as commander in chief, a president must maintain a basic level of personal conduct required from all those he commands.

It was with the military that Clinton was most vulnerable and, institutionally, did the most damage. As commander in chief of the armed forces and chief law enforcement officer, to perform well in that capacity requires at least the same basic level of personal conduct as those under the president's command. Robert Patterson served as the military aide to Clinton from May 1996 to May 1998. His primary duty was carrying the "football," the device necessary to launch a nuclear attack. Thus, Patterson spent virtually every day within just a matter of steps from President Clinton. He arrived in this position filled with professional devotion and commitment to serve. He left "disillusioned and disheartened."[68] Patterson explicitly states that life in the military was conducted at a far higher moral level than it was in the Clinton White House. "Clinton's primary downfall as commander in chief," according to Patterson, "was his inability to bridge the gap between legal authority and moral authority. Legal authority resides in the president's constitutional rights as the commander in chief. Legal authority was his from the outset. But his moral authority was shot almost from the outset."[69] In the end, Patterson was left with the sense that "the man in the Oval Office had sown a whirlwind of destruction upon the integrity of our government, endangered our national security, and done enormous harm to the American military in which [he] served."[70]

Finally, the problem with the argument that private character does not impact governing is that it ignores the health of the polity. As Bennett argues, "these arguments define us down; they assume a lower common denominator of behavior and leadership than we Americans ought to accept. And if we do accept it, we will have committed an unthinking act of moral and intellectual disarmament."[71]

Impeachment

Much of the same logic follows in terms of the public's general reactions to the impeachment process. Once again, Stanley Renshon provides a thoughtful analysis. He offers six broad explanations for the public's response to Clinton's impeachment—prior knowledge and thus prior acceptance of his character flaws, general public ambivalence, lower moral expectations of leaders, decline of public trust in government, the decline of public attention to politics in general, and the ultimate distinction between public and private behavior. [72]

Renshon also thinks that the public largely thought the impeachment process was built on issues of sexual inappropriateness rather than criminal behavior. He claims that a critical turning point was the release of the president's videotaped grand jury testimony in September 1998. Many felt the questioning was too intense and too sexually explicit. Polls reflected the view that committee members were prying into private matters. As a result, the general public tended to consider the controversy a private morality issue, not a public performance one.[73]

But where was the outrage? Where were the calls for resignation? Again, Renshon suggests several reasons not only why there was no public outcry for impeachment, but also why Clinton survived and actually gained public support during the ordeal. First, he suggests that whatever anger the public shared against Clinton, it was tempered by the weariness with all the personal attacks. Second, the public was reluctant to pass harsh judgment because of the state of the economy: low unemployment, low inflation, and a soaring stock market. Third, Renshon suggests Clinton's 1998 State of the Union address, viewed by more than 75 million Americans, provided an opportunity to provide the litany of accomplishments. Indeed, prior to the speech, Clinton's approval rating was 59 percent; after the speech, it rose to 67 percent. Before the speech, 44 percent of the public thought the country was heading in the right direction; after, 61 percent thought so. Thus, the speech provided momentary increases in personal support. Fourth, there were too many charges and allegations to follow and track, some very complicated. "The sheer number of legitimate ethical questions, actual and potential criminal indictments, and allegations (some serious, some marginal) surrounding the president and his administration made keeping up with them close to a full-time occupation."[74] Finally, perhaps Clinton simply represented the ethos of the baby-boomer generation. His actions and behavior simply reflected the attitudes and values of the times. After all, with infidelity and divorce running rampant, who wouldn't lie about an affair? Recall also the survey according to which the vast majority of young people did not consider oral sex as having sex.

So many observers, pundits, and academics reflecting upon the Clinton administration offer this latter point. They are quick to pronounce that Clinton was "just one of us," a mirror of the baby-boomer generation. Shawn and Trevor Parry-Giles share this pragmatic perspective. Post-impeachment, the nation needed to move on to the issues and business at hand and simply accept Clinton's "private foibles just as it had to accept the disappointments of a generation. Bill Clinton thus shouldered this cultural burden, complete with its headaches and its hopes. To convict Bill Clinton would be to condemn our past, our present, and our future."[75] As I have already revealed, this perspective simply cannot prevail if we are going to thrive as a democracy.

The Nixon Comparison

In my opinion, Clinton has damaged the presidency more than Nixon did. Nixon at least resigned. In terms of the case against Nixon, the simple facts are that he committed one public presidential lie, one invocation of presidential privilege, and no criminal offenses. Nixon never gave a single statement under oath during the Watergate affair.

Recall that it was the tapes that proved fatal to Nixon. The tapes recorded Nixon's discussion with John Dean detailing the payment of "hush" money to the burglars of the Democratic headquarters and ways to stop the FBI investigation. The latter he had vehemently denied in a nationally televised address. Conservative columnist James Kilpatrick wrote, upon the release of the tapes, "I am close to tears. My president is a liar. I wish he were a crook instead."[76]

Presidential scholar Aaron Wildavsky's observations about Nixon are clear. In 1975 he wrote, "President Nixon has done more to discredit our political institutions than any other person, group, or social movement in this century. All those bodies on all those lines by all those protestors all this past decade do not amount to a pinhead compared to what president Nixon had done all by himself in a year. He was elected to uphold America's institutions; instead he has worn them down."[77] Then, he observes, "If we could not trust the president, he had to go."[78]

Again, while discussing Nixon and the aftermath of Watergate, Wildavsky wrote on the importance of honesty and believing the president. "No human relationship can survive questioning the honesty and intent behind each any and every sentence."[79] He concludes, "The chief crime with which the president is charged is our inability to trust him, a serious, perhaps the most serious, public offense with which a political leader can be charged."[80]

The journalists who pursued the story behind Watergate, Bob Woodward and Carl Bernstein, wrote in 1976, "the problem is not Watergate or the cover-up. . . . It's that he hasn't been telling the truth to the American people. . . . The tape makes it evident that he hasn't leveled with the country for probably eighteen months. And the president can't lead a country he has deliberately misled for a year and a half."[81]

In the end, Nixon cared more about the public good than his self-pride. He cared more about the institutional presidency than his reputation. His resignation spared us the anguish of the trails of impeachment. There was some honor in his resignation. Nixon resigned in shame, but as Bennett observes, "Clinton's legacy is that he has no shame, no sense of duty or obligation to the country, and no concern for his own reputation."[82] From Marvin Olasky's perspective, for Clinton to show respect for the office "required confession and resignation, and that raising the bar in that fashion was more important than personal comfort, he would be handing his successors a presidency diminished by many of his actions but augmented by his last one."[83]

Pardons

Some of the same problematic "character" traits of Clinton were exhibited until the very end of his presidency. In the final hours, Clinton issued 140 pardons and commuted thirty-six prison sentences. Television commentator John McLaughlin lamented, "Not since the opening of the gates of the Bastille have so many criminals been liberated on a single day."[84] Some names were well known, such as Susan McDougal, Henry Cisneros, Patricia Hearst Shaw, and even Clinton's brother Roger. However, there were other less-known folks such as Susan Rosenberg, former member of the Weather underground terrorist group who participated in a 1981 Brinks robbery that left a guard and two police officers dead. Department of Justice pardon attorney Roger Adams stated that not only had many of the people on the list not applied for pardons, but there was no time to conduct record checks with the FBI as was the norm.

The media tended to focus on the pardons of Marc Rich and Pincus Green. They were charged with the largest tax-evasion scheme in American history. Between 1983 and 1984, the government filed a sixty-five-count indictment. Among the charges were wire fraud, mail fraud, racketeering, tax evasion (for $48 million), and trading with the enemy (Iran during the hostage crisis of 1979). Rather than face trial, they fled to Switzerland. They later became citizens of Spain and Israel. Denise Rich, Marc Rich's ex-wife, personally met with Clinton to discuss the pardons. Over the years, she had contributed more than $1 million to the Democratic Party, nearly half a million to Clinton's presidential library in Little Rock, $109,000 for Hillary Clinton's Senate campaign, $10,000 for Clinton's defense fund, and nearly $10,000 worth of furniture.[85]

Other ethical questions were raised because of the number of Clinton's family members and in-laws who were involved in some of the pardons. Hugh Rodham, Clinton's brother-in-law, received $400,000 for helping to obtain clemency for two felons. Tony Rodham, another brother-in-law, helped obtain a pardon for a couple. Even Clinton's brother, Roger, got in on the act. According to media accounts, he accepted money in exchange for promising pardons to two of his friends convicted of drug offenses.[86]

In the aftermath of the controversial number of individual presidential pardons by Clinton, he stated in an op-ed piece in the *New York Times*, "Overwhelmingly, the pardon went to people who had been convicted and served their time."[87] Of course, Marc Rich, for example, had not been convicted nor had he served time. Clinton also claimed the pardons were reviewed by three distinguished Republican attorneys. Within hours they all denied any involvement or review of cases.[88]

The Grand Exit

The Clintons left the White House with nearly $1 million in unreported gifts. There were thousands of dollars in jewelry, rugs, and furnishings, even unique gifts like a $90,000 framed handwritten letter by President Harry Truman and a rare 1952 Mickey Mantle baseball card worth $10,000. They received over $50,000 worth of china and flatware resulting from open solicitations by friends. In addition, all the gifts had to be "certified" before Hillary Clinton took office in the Senate. Senate gift rules limit her to $100 per year, per donor. All of this in light of her $8 million book advance. However, according to the Clintons, many gifts were not disclosed because they were turned over to Clinton's presidential library. Among the gift givers were several individuals connected to campaign finance violations and pardon supplicants.[89]

Then there were questions of "looting the White House." According to Barbara Olson, "while still in office, Bill and Hillary shipped 77 museum pieces, donated to the White House by prominent American artists, to the Clinton Presidential Library in Little Rock."[90] They also shipped furniture to their private residence in New York, which the White House chief usher raised concerns about. The items were donated as part of a $396,000 White House redecoration project in 1993. Ultimately, a truckload of couches, lamps, and other furnishings were returned.[91]

Historically, former presidents gracefully stepped back out of the limelight, especially during the first year of a new presidential term. This certainly was not the case for Clinton. In his last weekly radio address, Clinton promised to "work until the last hour of the last day." Upon departing Washington after the inauguration of George W. Bush, he promised a group of supporters at the airport, "I'm not going anywhere." In the first fourteen months after leaving office, Clinton had delivered over two hundred speeches in thirty different countries. Overseas, each speech was worth between $200,000 to $300,000; at home, at least $125,000. In addition to his annual speaking income of nearly $15 million, he received an advance of $12 million for his memoir, the largest nonfiction book deal in history.[92]

Clinton's post-presidency media coverage in both broadcast and print even rivaled the new president, George W. Bush. The magnitude of media coverage becomes even more impressive when comparing coverage of Clinton the first year upon leaving office with that of former president George H. W. Bush during the same period. According to the Center for Media and Public Affairs, from January 21, 2001, until February 28, 2001, a total of 101 stories about Clinton appeared on the nightly network newscasts, compared to only 14 stories for George H. W. Bush during the same timeframe in 1993.[93] In fact, for the first year out of office, Clinton received 260 minutes of airtime on the networks' evening news programs, compared to just 16 minutes for George H. W. Bush and 141 minutes for Reagan.[94] In the *New York Times* alone, Clinton appeared in 174 stories the first year out, compared to 49 stories for George H. W. Bush and 85 for Reagan.[95] Lori Han and Matthew Krov suggest three primary reasons for the difference in coverage. First, Clinton, at age fifty-four, was one of the youngest presidents to leave office since 1909. Thus, there was much curiosity of what he would do in the future. Second, Hillary's election to the U.S. Senate in 2000 kept him connected to the Washington scene. Finally, they suggest that the sheer number of continuing scandals and controversies surrounding him and his departure from office generated media interest. They conclude, "The American press has always enjoyed a good story, and as such, Clinton is perhaps the most newsworthy ex-president in American history."[96]

Implications

There are clear implications for future presidents. Based upon the public's acquittal and forgiveness of Clinton's misdeeds, future presidents will have several strategies to use when in trouble. First is the "popularity defense." As long as one's popularity stays high, the political risk of "punishment" is less. Second is the "privacy defense," the distinction between private and public behavior. Third, the "partisan defense." Any criticism, observation, or challenge is reduced to cries of partisan complaints, "attacks of personal destruction" without validity or acknowledgment.

Clinton did not exercise leadership, but impression management. He sought to bolster his charismatic and inspirational image. Impression management leaders stretch the facts to make themselves appear more confident and competent than they are, exaggerate accomplishments and past acts, project an image of greater personal strength and decisiveness than behavior warrants, and emphasize good points to the ignoring of shortcomings. This form of populist leadership must find ways for the public to identify with the leaders, usually by focusing on their humble backgrounds.

They also appeal to the current whims and opinions of the public, espouse values culled from polls, and pander to a factitious vision of the public's future. Richard Reeves characterizes Clinton as "a complete democrat, ever ready to change course to tack with the opinion of the great American public—as it drifts or lurches one way or another. Bill Clinton could be called the first true president of a new American public opinion democracy, acting as a facilitator for the wobbly will of the people."[97]

Legacy

So, what do we make of Bill Clinton as president? What will be his legacy? For political observer J. T. Young, what may well become Clinton's greatest legacy "is the fact that he has administered the first small presidency in the country's modern era. . . . Clinton is likely to share Grant's and Harding's historical fate. Despite peace and prosperity, neither of these presidents has received credit from history for the times over which he presided. While they undoubtedly received the momentary electoral benefits of good times, no one now credits them with having had a substantial hand in causing them."[98]

John Harris thinks the Clinton presidency "should be understood as an exercise in perpetual reinvention—a constantly evolving response to new circumstances and to new emergencies threatening his political survival. He executed this feat by using, to a degree unmatched by any predecessor, the modern techniques for managing public opinion: polling, advertising, and constant recalibration of presidential rhetoric."[99]

Noted presidential historian Stephen Wayne predicts that "when historians look back on the Clinton presidency, they may be more fascinated by Clinton himself than by the accomplishments and failures of his administration, the impact of his foreign and domestic policy on the country, or even his impeachment and its implications for the presidency. In short, the most enduring legacy of the Clinton years may very well be his character, his style, and his resiliency in the face of the crises he has faced in office."[100]

From a communication perspective, Joseph Blaney and William Benoit conclude that although Clinton is a gifted and effective communicator, "we have found his means of defense highly immoral ever since he entered the national spotlight as a candidate for the Democratic nomination for the presidency. He has shown repeatedly that he is willing to: omit material facts, bend the meaning of specific terms incredibly, engage in petty evasiveness, and lie explicitly." As their final observation, they state that "what is persuasive is not always right."[101]

On a more personal level, in comparison to Ronald Reagan, who was identified as a man of principle and admired for his pragmatic adaptations of his principles, Bruce Miroff thinks Clinton was "a shape-shifter on many of the major public issues during his presidency. His political identity, associated with the lower arts of political maneuver ('Slick Willie') and not the higher purposes of public philosophy, lacks symbolic resonance."[102]

Finally, journalist Joe Klein provides a somewhat social measure of Clinton's contemporary legacy.[103] A year after Clinton left office, there were only three quotations worthy enough to be included in the seventeenth edition of *Bartlett's Familiar Quotations*:

> "I experimented with marijuana a time or two. And I didn't like it, and didn't inhale, and didn't try it again."—3/31/92
>
> "I am going to say this again: I did not have sexual relations with that woman—Miss Lewinsky."—1/26/98
>
> "It depends on what the meaning of the word 'is' is. If the—if he—if 'is' means is and never has been, that is not—that is one thing. If it means there is none, that was a completely true statement."—8/17/98

For a person who was in office eight years, averaging more than 550 public speeches per year, the three quotes offer some legacy!

CONCLUSION

There are quantitative ways to judge the ethics of the Clinton administration. First, the number of independent counsels appointed is unprecedented for any administration. Second, the number of high-level officials who resigned while under an ethical cloud was an all-time high. Third, the number of days a story on the ethics of the administration was featured on the front page of major daily newspapers is historic in scope.

It is important to understand the historical significance of the Lewinsky episode. From Washington to George W. Bush, no sitting president had ever been indicted for a criminal offense. Remember that Nixon was named as "coconspirator." Clinton was just the second president to be impeached. No president until Clinton has been fined resulting from being held in contempt of court. No sitting president was sued to lose his license to practice law (although Nixon was disbarred after office in New York).

Stuart Taylor observes, "even more damaging that these crimes were Clinton's succession of lies to the American people; his abuse of the powers and privileges of his office to promote his lies; his vicious attacks (mostly through subordinates and surrogates) on truth-seekers such as Linda Tripp; and his efforts—aided and abetted by media apologists and by political propagandists posing as professors—to devalue the long-established principle that lying under oath is a serious crime."[104]

Bill Clinton's repeated betrayal of public trust had a profound impact on our political and civic culture. His administration contributed to the continued decline and trust of government and elected officials, only to be restored in large measure by President George W. Bush, at least initially and through the horrors of 9/11. Without trust, presidents may win office, but they cannot effectively govern. The problem is not one of *legality*, but *legitimacy*. When citizens become less trusting, it makes it difficult for future presidents to restore trust. "Ultimately," as Stanley Renshon observes, "the fabric of democracy is in danger as the psychological adhesive that holds it together loosens."[105]

For me, the fundamental question is whether the Clinton administration enhanced the public's confidence in the integrity of the federal government or instead caused further erosion of the public's trust. I think it did the latter. My overall conclusion about the ethics of the Clinton administration is that it regularly failed to live up to the maxim that public service is a public trust. In numerous situations, the White House took some actions, failed to take other actions, and made statements that would cause one to question the basic integrity of the Clinton administration.

NOTES

1. Shawn Parry-Giles and Trevor Parry-Giles, *Constructing Clinton* (New York: Peter Lang, 2002), 202.
2. Bruce Miroff, "From 'Midcentury' to Fin-de-Siecle: The Exhaustion of the Presidential Image," *Rhetoric & Public Affairs*, 1 (2), 1998, 196.
3. William J. Bennett, *The Death of Outrage* (New York: Free Press, 1998), 10.
4. Marvin Olasky, *The Leadership Tradition* (New York: Free Press, 1999), 271.
5. George Stephanopoulos, *All Too Human* (Boston: Little, Brown, 1999), 4.
6. Stephanopoulos, *All Too Human*, 5.
7. Bennett, *The Death of Outrage*, 5.
8. Stanley Renshon, *High Hopes: The Clinton Presidency and the Politics of Ambition* (New York: New York University Press, 1996), xi.

9. Robert Shogan, *The Double-Edged Sword* (Boulder, CO: Westview, 2000), 223.
10. J. T. Young, "Clinton in Context: A Look at the Man and the Presidency," *World and I*, 15, 2000, 326.
11. Martha J. Kumar, "President Clinton Meets the Media: Communications Shaped by Predictable Patterns," in *The Clinton Presidency*, Stanley Renshon, ed. (Boulder, CO: Westview, 1995), 177.
12. Paul Greenberg, *No Surprises* (Washington, DC: Brassey's, 1996), viii.
13. Susan Schmidt and Michael Weisskopf, *Truth at Any Cost* (New York: HarperCollins, 2001), 119.
14. Sidney Blumenthal, *The Clinton Wars* (New York: Farrar, Straus and Giroux, 2003), 462–63.
15. Blumenthal, *Clinton Wars*, 464–65.
16. James Bovard, "*Feeling Your Pain*" (New York: St. Martin's Press, 2000), 347.
17. Olasky, *The Leadership Tradition*, 263.
18. Stuart Taylor, "How Clinton Trashed the Constitution to Save It," *National Journal*, 33 (4), January 27, 2001, 242.
19. Stanley Renshon, "The Public's Response to the Clinton Scandals, Part 1," *Presidential Studies Quarterly*, 32 (1), 2002, 170.
20. Renshon, "The Public's Response to the Clinton Scandals, Part 1," 275.
21. Stanley Renshon, "The Public's Response to the Clinton Scandals, Part 2," *Presidential Studies Quarterly*, 32 (2), 2002, 422.
22. Renshon, "The Public's Response to the Clinton Scandals, Part 1," 242.
23. Shogan, *The Double-Edged Sword*, 272.
24. Christopher Hitchens, *No One Left to Lie To* (New York: Verso, 1999), 24.
25. Ann Coulter, *High Crimes and Misdemeanors* (Washington, DC: Regnery, 1998), 113.
26. Greenberg, *No Surprises*, 299.
27. Colin Campbell and Bert Rockman, "Preface," in *The Clinton Legacy*, Colin Campbell and Bert Rockman, eds. (New York: Chatham House, 2000), xii.
28. Robert Patterson, *Dereliction of Duty* (Washington, DC: Regnery, 2003), 51.
29. Rich Lowry, *Legacy: Paying the Price for the Clinton Years* (Washington, DC: Regnery, 2003), 145.
30. Renshon, *High Hopes*, 70.
31. Renshon, *High Hopes*, 131.
32. Bruce Miroff, "Courting the Public," in *The Postmodern Presidency*, Steven Schier, ed. (Pittsburgh: University of Pittsburgh Press, 2000), 108.
33. Bert Rockman, "Cutting *With* the Grain: Is There a Clinton Leadership Legacy?" in *The Clinton Legacy*, Colin Campbell and Bert Rockman, eds. (New York: Chatham House, 2000), 284.
34. Lowry, *Legacy*, 6.
35. Lowry, *Legacy*, 50.

36. Stanley Renshon, "Character, Judgment, and Political Leadership," in *The Clinton Presidency*, Stanley Renshon, ed. (Boulder, CO: Westview, 1995), 74–75.

37. Stephen Wayne, "Presidential Personality: The Clinton Legacy," in *The Clinton Scandal and the Future of American Government*, Mark Rozell and Clyde Wilcox, eds. (Washington, DC: Georgetown University Press, 2000), 218.

38. Louis Fisher, "When Presidential Power Backfires: Clinton's Use of Clemency," *Presidential Studies Quarterly*, 32 (3), 2002, 596.

39. Renshon, "Character, Judgment, and Political Leadership," 77.

40. Lowry, *Legacy*, 5.

41. Renshon, "Character, Judgment, and Political Leadership," 77.

42. Greenberg, *No Surprises*, xii–xiv.

43. Greenberg, *No Surprises*, 1.

44. Elizabeth Drew, *On the Edge* (New York: Simon & Schuster, 1994), 395–96.

45. Renshon, *High Hopes*, 37.

46. Greenberg, *No Surprises*, 74.

47. Renshon, *High Hopes*, 83.

48. Renshon, *High Hopes*, 84.

49. Greenberg, *No Surprises*, xiv.

50. Drew, *On the Edge*, 418.

51. Renshon, "Character, Judgment, and Political Leadership," 77.

52. As quoted in Bennett, *The Death of Outrage*, 46.

53. As quoted in Bennett, *The Death of Outrage*, 47.

54. Howard Kurtz, *Spin Cycle: Inside the Clinton Propaganda Machine* (New York: Free Press, 1998), 203.

55. Diane J. Heith, "Polling for a Defense," *Presidential Studies Quarterly*, 30 (4), 2000, 783–84.

56. Heith, "Polling for a Defense," 785.

57. Graham Wilson, "Clinton in Comparative Perspective," in *The Clinton Legacy*, Colin Campbell and Bert Rockman, eds. (New York: Chatham House, 2000), 254.

58. Heith, "Polling for a Defense," 786–87.

59. Heith, "Polling for a Defense," 789.

60. Renshon, "The Public's Response to the Clinton Scandals, Part 1," 176.

61. Bruce Miroff, "The Contemporary Presidency: Moral Character in the White House," *Presidential Studies Quarterly*, 29 (3), 1999, 708.

62. Richard Pious, "The Paradox of Clinton Winning and the Presidency Losing," *Political Science Quarterly*, 114, 1999, 569.

63. Greenberg, *No Surprises*, 23.

64. Diane Harvey, "The Public's View of Clinton," in *The Postmodern Presidency*, Steven Schier, ed. (Pittsburgh: University of Pittsburgh Press, 2000), 142.

65. "When he unleashed the Air Force to punish Saddam Hussein, his critics charged him with manipulating the crisis to preserve his political skin. Unwilling to take the political risk of sending ground troops to fight the Serbian armies of Slobadan Milosovic, Clinton relied solely on bombing the Serbs into submission. As a result, he was unable to prevent 1.5 million Kosovars, on whose behalf the war had supposedly been fought, from being driven from their homes." Shogan, *The Double-Edged Sword*, 280.

66. Shogan, *The Double-Edged Sword*, 227.

67. Campbell and Rockman, "Preface," xii–xiii.

68. Patterson, *Dereliction of Duty*, 19.

69. Patterson, *Dereliction of Duty*, 95.

70. Patterson, *Dereliction of Duty*, 147.

71. Bennett, *The Death of Outrage*, 9.

72. Renshon, "The Public's Response to the Clinton Scandals, Part 1," 182.

73. Renshon, "The Public's Response to the Clinton Scandals, Part 1," 181.

74. Renshon, "The Public's Response to the Clinton Scandals, Part 2," 417.

75. Parry-Giles and Parry-Giles, *Constructing Clinton*, 177.

76. Stanley Kulter, *The Wars of Watergate* (New York: Alfred A. Knopf, 1990), 54.

77. Aaron Wildavsky, *The Beleaguered Presidency* (New Brunswick, NJ: Transaction, 1991), 165.

78. Wildavsky, *The Beleaguered Presidency*, 166.

79. Wildavsky, *The Beleaguered Presidency*, 168.

80. Wildavsky, *The Beleaguered Presidency*, 170.

81. Bob Woodward and Carl Bernstein, "The Final Days: Part Two," *Newsweek*, April 12, 1976.

82. Bennett, *The Death of Outrage*, 106.

83. Olasky, *The Leadership Tradition*, 271.

84. Barbara Olson, *The Final Days* (Washington, DC: Regnery, 2001), 10.

85. Fisher, "When Presidential Power Backfires," 586–99.

86. Fisher, "When Presidential Power Backfires," 595.

87. Fisher, "When Presidential Power Backfires," 595.

88. Fisher, "When Presidential Power Backfires," 595.

89. Olson, *The Final Days*, 69.

90. Olson, *The Final Days*, 71–72.

91. Olson, *The Final Days*, 71.

92. Jonathan Alter, "Citizen Clinton Up Close," *Newsweek*, April 8, 2002, 36.

93. Lori Han and Matthew Krov, "Out of Office and in the News," *Presidential Studies Quarterly*, 33 (4) (2003), 926.

94. Han and Krov, "Out of Office and in the News," 930.

95. Han and Krov, "Out of Office and in the News," 927.

96. Han and Krov, "Out of Office and in the News," 931.

97. Richard Reeves, *Running in Place* (Kansas City, KS: Andrews and McMeel, 1966), 10–11.
98. J. T. Young, "Clinton in Context," 339.
99. John Harris, "A Clouded Mirror," in *The Postmodern Presidency,* Steven Schier, ed. (Pittsburgh: University of Pittsburgh Press, 2000), 88.
100. Wayne, "Presidential Personality," 211.
101. Joseph Blaney and William Benoit, *The Clinton Scandals and the Politics of Image Restoration* (Westport, CT: Praeger, 2001), 147.
102. Miroff, "Courting the Public," 111.
103. Joe Klein, *The Natural* (New York: Doubleday, 2002), 11.
104. Taylor, "How Clinton Trashed the Constitution to Save It," 243.
105. Renshon, *High Hopes,* 10–11.

6

So, What About
George W. Bush?

*In America's ideal of freedom, the public interest depends on
private character, on integrity and tolerance toward others and
the rule of conscience in our own lives.*

—GEORGE W. BUSH

The 2000 presidential campaign will most likely be remembered for
what happened after the polls closed on November 7 rather than for
the speeches, conventions, issues, debates, or television ads. On Election
Day, no one expected the outcome of the race would take thirty-six days,
more than fifty lawsuits, and a Supreme Court ruling.

However, personal character was an underlying theme to the Bush
2000 presidential campaign. Upon making his presidential campaign
announcement, George W. Bush promised "a new responsibility era" in
which "each American must understand that we are responsible for the
decisions that each of us makes in life." In his first appearance in New
Hampshire, Bush stated, "I think it's important for any of us who assume
high office to understand that when we put our hand on the Bible, that
we're swearing not only to uphold the laws of the land, but that we are
swearing to uphold the dignity of the office to which we've been elected."[1]

Bush openly invited the comparison and contrast to Clinton. He frequently ended campaign stump speeches by raising his right hand and
pledging "to uphold the honor and dignity of the office of the president."

However, there was one event, late in the campaign, that questioned
Bush's integrity and character. Just five days before the election, two Portland

89

television stations, WPXT and WCSH, reported that in 1976 George W. Bush was arrested and convicted of driving under the influence of alcohol.

THE DUI INCIDENT

The details revealed that shortly after midnight on September 4, 1976, George W. Bush was driving on Ocean Avenue in Kennebunkport, Maine, to his family's summer home. Earlier that evening, Bush, along with his seventeen-year-old sister Dorothy, Australian tennis star John Newcombe and his wife, and family friend Pete Roussel, had been drinking beer at a local bar. Police officer Calvin Bridges pulled Bush over when he saw the car go onto the shoulder and then back onto the road. Bridges requested Bush to perform a roadside sobriety test, which he failed. Bush freely admitted to drinking and fully cooperated with Bridges. When asked about the incident twenty-four years later, retired Bridges responded, "The man was, and I say this without being facetious, a picture of integrity. He gave no resistance. He was very cooperative."[2]

Bush was arrested on the scene and escorted to the police station, where he failed an alcohol level test, scoring 0.12, which is over Maine's then legal limit of 0.10. Bush was released from the police station on $500 bail and later pleaded guilty for the misdemeanor, which resulted in a $150 fine and a short suspension of his driving privileges in Maine.[3]

The story and subsequent admission became the center of national media attention. In what was already a tightening race, the revelation generated a crisis for the Bush campaign. As we now know, just a shift of a few thousand votes in Florida alone would have changed the outcome of the election. Even beyond Florida, there were six other states decided by very small vote margins.[4]

Throughout the campaign, there were persistent rumors about Bush's drug use in college, primarily cocaine, and his wild parties involving plenty of drinking. Classmates characterized him as a "party boy." In fact, the 1976 DUI arrest was not his first. In 1966, Bush and some of his fraternity brothers were arrested for stealing a Christmas wreath, but the charges were later dropped.[5] In addition, four years prior to the Kennebunkport arrest, Bush was driving home from a Washington party with his fifteen-year-old brother, Marvin, when he ran over a neighbor's trash can and dragged it down the street. Upon arriving home, he and his father got into a heated "discussion."[6]

During his campaigns for governor of Texas as well as for president, Bush declined to answer any direct statements about his past, whether it was about drinking, drugs, or prior arrests. For example, in 1996 Bush was summoned to jury duty in Austin for a DUI case and was taken off the panel of potential jurors early in the selection process. As Bush left the courtroom, reporters asked if he had ever been arrested for a DUI. He answered, "I do not have a perfect record as a youth." When asked if that response was a yes or no, Bush replied, "When I was young, I did a lot of foolish things."[7]

Also, on the jury duty forms in 1996, eleven of the thirty-eight questions were not completed, including one about prior arrests. The reason given was that a staffer completed the form and did not know the information, and thus left the items unanswered.[8]

When all the questions arose again during the 2000 presidential campaign, Bush's standard response was "When I was young and irresponsible, I was young and irresponsible." One other time, Bush did say he could indeed meet FBI background questions about drug use. In the strictest sense, this meant Bush had not used drugs for at least the last seven years. The next day Bush expanded his claim. Not only could he meet the Clinton White House standard, he could also meet his father's 1989 more stringent standard of no drug use within the last fifteen years. For Bush, that meant at least no drug use since he was twenty-eight years old.[9] For what it is worth, vice presidential nominee Dick Cheney was convicted for two DUIs during his twenties.[10]

The first major response came that evening from Bush himself at 9:16 p.m. (ET). His statement was simple and straightforward:

> There's a report out tonight that 24 years ago I was apprehended in Kennebunkport, Maine, for a DUI. That's an accurate story. I'm not proud of that. I oftentimes said that years ago I made some mistakes. I occasionally drank too much and I did that night. I was pulled over. I admitted to the policeman that I had been drinking. I paid a fine. And I regret it happened. But it did. I've learned my lesson. As I mentioned, I—as many of you know that I quit drinking alcohol in 1986. And it was the right decision for me to make then. I would be glad to answer a few questions.[11]

The crisis for the campaign was obvious. Was the failure to disclose the arrest and conviction of DUI an act of deception? After all, as already mentioned, a major thrust of the campaign, even more so than specific issues, was to portray Bush as a direct opposite of Clinton in terms of integrity, honesty, and trustworthiness. Would the disclosure damage his carefully constructed image, resulting in loss of support and votes?

Upon the announcement, both campaigns were uncertain about the impact of the story. Some thought the report did not reveal anything new about Bush's past; he had already confessed to problems with alcohol. Others thought it would hurt Bush's electoral efforts because it would question his candor, credibility, and hence trustworthiness, all positive traits stressed during the campaign.[12]

Without question, most communication specialists concede that the arrest should have been disclosed, if not during his gubernatorial campaigns, at least very early in the presidential primary season. As James Ceasar and Andrew Busch observe, "He created an unnecessary vulnerability for himself that allowed a negative story to dominate two or three days of the news during the final week of the campaign."[13]

Several of Bush's campaign advisors knew of the arrest and conviction.[14] However, despite their advice, he refused to make the information public because of the potential impact upon his daughters. Bush had counseled them not to drink and drive. His disclosure would provide the wrong message for his daughters, not to mention his personal embarrassment.

In this crisis, it was important to bolster the characteristics of honesty, trustworthiness, and candor as well as to reiterate the general good personal traits of Bush. The campaign attempted to reduce the importance and magnitude of the incident by noting that the incident was twenty-four years old, that Bush no longer drinks alcoholic beverages, and that his primary concerns all along were his daughters and his role as father. And implied attacks on the Gore campaign gained credibility given the timing and source of the revelation.

Gore personally refused to comment on the matter, stating he would not engage in "personal attacks."[15] However, his campaign chairperson, William Daley, provided a press release stating that the campaign had nothing to do with the release of the information. "This charge is wrong. It is made without proof or evidence. We categorically deny any involvement. Charges to the contrary are irresponsible. It is time for Governor Bush's campaign to stop hurling charges, and start accepting responsibility. Whatever questions remain unanswered are the responsibility of Governor Bush and his campaign, not ours."[16]

As already mentioned, neither campaign was sure of the potential impact of the DUI announcement. After a couple days of media frenzy, opinions and observations ranged from little to no negative impact upon Bush to some speculating the episode could actually help Bush. For others, the incident could either benefit or hurt Gore. Thus, there were comments, observations, and opinions representing virtually all possible scenarios, impacts, and outcomes.

Initially, Bush was portrayed as at best a hypocrite and at worst a liar. From the beginning of his campaign, Bush contrasted his personal character to that of both Clinton and Gore. However, on issues of drugs and "youthful discretions," Bush would always be evasive, never being specific as to past problems or events. The obvious danger to Bush with the election just days away was losing support from independent and swing voters or motivating them to stay home, feeding the already prevalent "politics as usual" cynicism. From a more pragmatic perspective, not only did the story dominate the headlines for days, forcing both campaigns off message, there was also the genuine fear among the Bush staff that the story would open the door to further investigations and questions of his past.

For some strategists, Bush had already inoculated himself from the issue by acknowledging some past alcohol abuse and the decision to stop drinking at age forty. However, the strongest benefit to Bush was for the disclosure to be portrayed as an obvious "dirty trick" by the Gore campaign. The story reinforced the claim that Gore would "do or say anything" to get elected. Of course, silently the Gore campaign hoped the disclosure would energize Democrats, eliminate the "character issue," and actually demonstrate that Bush was "not ready for prime time."

As soon as the story broke, traditional media and especially cable news channels went into a frenzy covering the story. As a result of the disclosure, news about the DUI conviction stimulated stories focusing on Bush's character once again. In fact, his character was raised twice as frequently during the final days of the campaign as it had been during the entire week of the Republican convention.[17]

Most opinion polls following the announcement of the DUI conviction and Bush's response revealed that between 8 and 10 percent of "likely voters" were *less likely* to vote for him. In contrast, between 75 and 85 percent indicated that the report would have no effect one way or another, while approximately 15 percent thought the incident actually increased Bush's credibility. Bush maintained a slight lead in every tracking poll during the period leading up to Election Day.[18] In a *USA Today* poll, 41 percent of "likely voters" thought the disclosure was in fact "a dirty trick."[19] Thus, from a macro perspective, the DUI announcement appeared to do little damage to the Bush campaign. However, as we now know, given the dynamics of the race, the loss of 8 to 10 percent of the voters could well have impacted the outcome in not only several battleground states but in the election itself.

In general, the public did not seem to hold Bush accountable or responsible for the crisis. In terms of the issue of alcohol abuse, Bush had inoculated himself throughout the campaign by acknowledging that he had made unwise decisions when young and at age forty stopped drinking.

Recall that while appearing on *Oprah* in September 2000, Bush stated, "Alcohol was beginning to compete for my affections, compete for my affection for my wife and family. It was starting to crowd out my energy and I just had to quit."[20]

Another factor that minimized the impact of the crisis upon the Bush campaign is what I call the "Clinton factor." Bush was indeed successful in presenting himself in direct contrast to the personal characteristics of Bill Clinton. According to qualities that mattered most to voters, Bush was perceived as more honest and trustworthy by 80 percent to Gore's 15 percent and more likeable by 59 percent to Gore's 38 percent. In contrast, Gore was perceived as having more experience by 82 percent to Bush's 17 percent, having a better understanding of issues by 75 percent to Bush's 19 percent, and caring more about people by 63 percent to Bush's 31 percent.[21]

In addition, the public was tired of scandal, and the nature of the DUI disclosure hinted strongly as a "dirty trick." There is no question that Clinton's legacy of scandals hurt Gore. Among the twenty-five battleground states, the large majority of voters who disapproved of job performance and personally disliked Clinton supported Bush. His percentage of support ranged from 83 percent to 92 percent of those voters. Even those who approved of Clinton's job performance but personally disliked him supported Bush, ranging from 26 percent to 44 percent.[22] A *Los Angeles Times* poll revealed that a full 30 percent of those who voted for Bush indicated that "disapproval of Clinton's personal behavior" had a major influence on their vote.[23]

Although just a footnote to the 2000 presidential contest, the disclosure of Bush's DUI arrest and conviction did undoubtedly impact the campaign. By the 2004 presidential contest, chief strategist Karl Rove acknowledged that the DUI announcement kept at least three to four million evangelicals at home. Not only did the announcement cost Bush a majority of the vote, it almost cost him the presidency.

Although in truth it is difficult to assess the full impact, it is safe to conclude that the impact was not as harmful as it could have been given the strategic management of the crisis, Bush's established images being consistent with the information about the DUI, and the lingering influence of Clinton's legacy of scandal.

According to political scientist Gary Jacobson, the 2000 presidential election culminated three decades of growing partisan polarization among both American politicians and voters. "By every measure, politics in Washington had become increasingly polarized along partisan and ideological lines in the decades between the Nixon and Clinton administrations."[24]

THE CHARACTER OF GEORGE W. BUSH

George Bush began his presidency with very little political capital, the least since Gerald Ford, who assumed the office without a single popular vote. However, the lack of an electoral mandate did not prevent Bush from pursuing his agenda. By the end of his first six months in office, President Bush had won his tax cuts and well established a conservative legislative agenda.[25] He did it by "strengthening his own political base, speaking from conviction, advancing serious policy ideas, and doing it all with a smile on his face."[26]

Bush came to office with a rather stable public image and persona. He was viewed as personable, honorable, decisive, and straightforward. However, on the somewhat negative perspective, he was also viewed as lacking native intelligence and curiosity. Indeed, the view of George Bush reflects our nearly evenly divided country. Those in the "red" (Bush) states see him as a confident, self-knowing, and steady commander in chief, while those mostly in the "blue" (2000 Gore/2004 Kerry) states see a cocksure bully who struts his power around the world.[27]

According to Chief of Staff Andrew Card, "You don't find a lot of nuance in what he says. . . . He's a tell-it-like-it-is person. He does not pick his words to obfuscate. A lot of diplomats will choose words to obfuscate. I think it goes back to Texas and Texas oilmen. He's from the rough-and-tumble world of Midland, Texas. Your word means more than the contract there. In Midland, when you shake hands, that means more than your signature on the contract."[28]

In a January 2001 NBC/*Wall Street Journal* poll that rated the incoming president's personal qualities, Bush rated best for "representing traditional American values," "having high personal standards that set the proper moral tone for the country," and "being easygoing and likeable."[29]

Even a casual reading of biographical material on George W. Bush reveals that his core values are family, faith, and integrity. Hugh Heclo claims that the fundamental ethos of Bush is that of his family. He grew up in a family of high expectations but also quick to deflate anyone puffing up his or her accomplishments. "The family wealth and ethos provided security, but not spoon-feeding. Though help was always available, each member of the family was expected to stand on his or her own two feet, yet no one was to behave in a prideful manner for doing so."[30] In fact, John Dilulio, former presidential assistant, thinks it is impossible to fully understand Bush's presidential character without fully appreciating his "small-d democratic" beliefs and sensibilities. "What Bush really dislikes are academic or other elites who, as I heard him phrase it on occasion, 'are' or 'come off' as 'smart without any heart,' who are 'down on average Americans' who 'just believe in this great country' and its 'great goodness.'"[31] For three generations of Bush men, public service meant political leadership.

What has become an apocalyptic story reveals a great deal about the character and motivation of George W. Bush. A week after his father was elected president in 1988, George W. Bush asked his friend and advisor Doug Wead, "What's going to happen to me?" Subsequently, Wead did some historical research on the lives of presidential children. He generated a forty-four-page memo entitled "All the President's Children." Wead discovered presidential offspring were generally burdened by high expectations but failure by comparison, lives of alcoholism and divorce, and premature death.[32] Over the next few years there was a genuine transformation of George Bush.

Friends and acquaintances indicate that the defining characteristics of George Bush, other than his faith, include discipline and competition. John Podhoretz argues that his presidential style is almost completely the reverse of Clinton. Clinton was daring in the way he pursued his personal hungers. In contract, George W. Bush has remarkable self-discipline in his personal life. "To a man, his close aides describe him as the most disciplined person they've ever known."[33] Again, Chief of Staff Card observes, "The president is a man of great discipline. . . . His discipline extends to every aspect of his life. His faith, his love for his family, doing his homework, making decisions, his health, what he eats, exercise, and getting sleep."[34] The Bush administration is characterized as being more professional, and being on time is simply mandatory. Being on time also reflects his sense of discipline.[35] Of course, critics view such discipline as evidence of rigidity of beliefs, attitudes, values, and behavior.

According to leadership scholars Carolyn Thompson and James Ware, when assembling his staff, Bush starts with core values. Those selected will mirror his beliefs. "He knows that getting all his team members on the same page enhances performance. Values drive behavior. He used this knowledge in choosing business partners, in governing Texas, and in running the country. Once Bush assembled a team that was clear about its core principles, his team was free to make decisions based on those principles."[36]

George Bush's very first act as president was to issue a specific set of ethical standards for all federal government employees. In the memorandum to employees, Bush stated, "Everyone who enters into public service for the United States has a duty to the American people to maintain the highest standards of integrity in government."[37]

Traditionally, character and integrity are reflected in day-to-day inter-actions, in private conversations and behaviors. With Bush, the change and contrast for White House staff and Secret Service members were instant. As one Secret Service agent revealed to Ronald Kessler, "He was punctual. Clinton was never on time for anything. It was embarrassing. Bush and his wife treated you normally, decently. They had conversations with us. The Clintons were arrogant, standoffish, and paranoid. Everyone got a morale boost with Bush. He was the complete opposite of Clinton."[38] Secret Service members and other staff of the White House report that Clinton generally ignored them or flew into rages over imag-ined failings. "If Clinton was nasty and temperamental, Hillary Clinton could make Richard Nixon look benign."[39] The Clintons were known for their temper tantrums throughout their eight years in the White House. In contrast, the Bushes remember the names of every staff member and the crew of Air Force One. They routinely thank staff members for every-day actions. Bush even plays baseball with members of the Secret Service and inquires about their families.[40]

Clinton's attitudes and style were also reflected in his White House staff. According to U.S. General Services Administration manager Lucille Price, "they didn't like to work. They didn't return calls. They were rude . . . they were the most unprofessional people I'd seen since I'd been here, which was since Gerald Ford."[41] In contrast, the Bush team is character-ized as competent, organized, and professional.

According to Bertram Brown, a psychiatrist and former head of the National Institute of Mental Health, observes that being president either creates or distorts character. Kessler argues that "unless a president comes to the office with good character and competence, the crushing force of the office and the adulation of the chief executive receives will inevitably lead to disaster."[42]

THE ATTACKS OF 9/11 AND THE IRAQ WAR

For most Americans and many others around the globe, life was sus-pended on September 11, 2001. The perpetrators gained our attention and that of the world. They took control of our public agenda and even our private lives. Fighter jets flew over major cities; Air Force One flew evasive patterns throughout the day and the Secret Service kept Vice President Cheney in virtual hiding.

On the evening of September 11, 2001, President George W. Bush acknowledged that "Today, our nation saw evil, the very worst of human nature."[43] Nine days later, before a joint session of Congress, President Bush proclaimed

> on September the eleventh, enemies of freedom committed an act of war against our country. Americans have known wars—but for the past 136 years, they have been wars on foreign soil, except for one Sunday in 1941. Americans have known the casualties of war—but not at the center of a great city on a peaceful morning. Americans have known surprise attacks—but never before on thousands of civilians. All of this was brought upon us in a single day—and night fell on a different world, a world where freedom itself is under attack.[44]

We were "at war." President Bush announced that "our war on terror begins with al-Qaida, but it does not end there. It will not end until every terrorist group of global reach has been found, stopped, and defeated."[45]

Not since the assassination of President John Kennedy had so many Americans and others around the world stayed glued to their television sets. For the first five days after the terrorist attack, television and radio networks covered the aftermath around the clock. All four of the major networks (i.e., ABC, CBS, FOX, and NBC) suspended regular programming and provided ninety hours of "wall to wall" coverage, exceeding the amount devoted to President Kennedy's assassination in 1962 and the first Iraq war in 1991.[46] We followed the horror and minute-by-minute destruction of the World Trade Center buildings, people jumping to their deaths and running for their lives, the flames engulfing the Pentagon, and the Pennsylvania crash site of United Flight 93.

To be "at war" demands some form of action. At home, President Bush's early pronouncements acknowledged our shock, anger, and promise of justice. No surprise to historians or presidential scholars, there was a tremendous jump in Bush's approval rating in the aftermath of the attacks of 9/11. According to a Gallup poll, he went from a 51 percent approval rating on September 10 to an 86 percent rating on September 15, 2001. The thirty-five-point jump is the largest in the history of polling.[47] The percentage of Americans who viewed Bush as a strong and decisive leader rose from 55 percent to 75 percent after the attacks of 9/11. A Pew Research Center poll showed that 45 percent of Americans thought Bush proved to be a stronger leader than anticipated.[48] In addition, Bush enjoyed one of the longest stretches of popularity of any president since the inception of polling. For the rest of 2001, Bush's approval rating averaged 87 percent.

Thus, after the attacks, in a very short time, Bush did a credible job in uniting the country, mobilizing the military for action in Afghanistan, gaining support from the international community in preparation for retaliation, and laying the groundwork for addressing the various issues of homeland security.

However, the approach and execution of the Iraq war to remove Saddam Hussein was a very different experience for George Bush. Americans, as well as the rest of the world, were slow to support the war. The war in Iraq clearly divided the country, especially along partisan lines. Just prior to the war, 56 percent of Democrats disapproved of Bush's approach to Iraq, compared to just 15 percent of Republicans.[49]

As the Iraq war neared, journalists began to challenge not so much Bush's assumptions, but his core being, his religiosity. Joe Klein of *Time* magazine wrote, "What is disturbing about Bush's faith in the moment of crisis" is that "it does not discomfort him enough: it does not impel him to have second thoughts, to explore other intellectual possibilities or question the possible consequences of his actions. . . . George W. Bush's faith offers no speed bumps on the road to Baghdad."[50]

Among liberals and the mainstream press, the argument or assessment of Bush, according to John Podhoretz, stems from the simple notion of "privilege: non-achieving, smart-ass, goof-off drunk rich kid gets into National Guard with Daddy's help, shirks it while he's in there, gets set up in oil biz through Dad, fails, gets set up in baseball 'cause of Dad and rich benefactors who owe his dad, manages to turn $700,000 into $14 million . . . just gets, gets, gets throughout his life, and then to top it off, gets the effin' presidency even though he didn't really win."[51]

Literally, with each passing month from 9/11, the anti-Bush rhetoric intensified and op-eds became critical and judgmental. Harold Meyerson, columnist for the *Washington Post*, summed it up in a cover article for the *American Prospect*: "He is incomparably more dangerous than Reagan or any other president in this nation's history."[52] Feel-good sites for Bush haters sprang up all over the web, with such names as Presidentmoron.com, Bushisamoron.com, and Toostupidtobepresident.com, to name just a few.[53]

By the summer of 2003, with Bush's poll numbers dropping, Democrats began to once again challenge Bush's legitimacy. Presidential candidate Carol Moseley Braun repeatedly proclaimed that Bush was not elected by the American people. Senator Tom Harkin of Iowa actually declared that Bush stole the election in 2000. By the autumn of 2003, liberals and Democrats proclaimed that Bush had consciously and with forethought deceived the American people to engage in war with

Iraq. Edward Kennedy stated publicly, "This was a made-up fraud. This was made up in Texas, announced in January [2003] to the Republican leadership that the war was going to take place and was going to be good politically."[54] Indeed, throughout 2003 and 2004, there were numerous comparisons of Bush to Hitler. The apparent hatred extended beyond the media and political rivals. At a presidential conference at Princeton University, numerous tenured professors in attendance not only were critical of Bush's policies, but personally ridiculed him and his Christian faith.[55] A summary of liberal, political, and several press charges against Bush includes: he is a moron; he is a puppet; he is a religious fanatic; he is Hitler, but not as talented; he is a "cowboy"; and he is certainly a liar.

Interestingly, Bush became even more polarizing than Bill Clinton. The gap between Bush's approval ratings for Republicans compared to Democrats was for several months the largest since Gallup has been measuring presidential approval.[56] As Gary Jacobson observed, "Despite Bush's national leadership in a time of crisis and widely popular military triumphs, his first thirty months in office have left the electorate, like the Congress, as divided and polarized as when he entered the White House."[57]

RELIGION, POLITICS, AND GEORGE W. BUSH

While religion has always been a part of American politics and presidents from the beginning of our nation have evoked the name of God, none have talked more or professed their religious faith with more vigor than George W. Bush.[58] Guy Lawson argues that "George W. Bush is the most overtly and publicly religious leader of the United States in generations. He speaks constantly of faith and the power of prayer and America's special place in the purposes of God. Religion permeates his official speeches and informal talks."[59] Throughout Bush's first term, he freely laces his speeches with phrases that echo familiar hymns and Bible verses.

Bush's faith was well known and on display even during the 2000 presidential campaign. In one of the debates, Bush identified Jesus Christ as his favorite political philosopher or thinker. Upon being asked to more fully explain his response, Bush said, "Well, if they don't know, it's going to be hard to explain. When you turn your heart and your life over to Christ, when you accept Christ as savior, it changes your heart. It changes your life."[60]

Richard Land, president of the Ethics and Religious Liberty Commission of the Southern Baptist Convention, is an advisor to the

White House and has known the president since 1988. He confirms that Bush "is an evangelical Christian, there is no doubt about that." This means, quite simply, that "he believes in the truth of the Bible with a capital *T*: the virgin birth, the death of Christ on the cross for our sins, the physical resurrection and, most importantly, a personal relationship with Jesus."[61] As already mentioned earlier, Bush reads the Bible daily, openly. He accepts Jesus Christ as his personal savior and attends the White House morning prayer meetings.

In a pre-election interview with Bill O'Reilly, President Bush stated, "Christ has influenced me, thanks to Billy Graham who planted a seed in my heart and it changed my life. It really did. I'm—I take great solace. I recognize I'm a humble—I'm a lowly sinner who sought redemption." When asked directly why he mentions his faith, Bush responded, "I really mention my faith vis-à-vis my life. And—I don't know—I don't know why people get upset with that. People—I'm asked the question, 'what does faith mean to me?' It means strength and calm in the face of a storm. I mean, I . . . I do rely on prayer and I . . . I am empowered by the fact—empowered by the fact that people pray for me. I'm sustained by that, not empowered. I'm sustained by that, it's a better word. I don't know why people object to somebody who is—when asked, says religion's important."[62]

In an interview, Raney Aronson, producer of PBS's *Frontline* program entitled "The Jesus Factor," concludes, "The president's face is very genuine. We thought at the end it's authentic. . . . I also think he very much believes that Jesus changed his heart. He believes he can do that for other people, too. . . . I did find an interesting sort of dichotomy in the way that people saw his faith. People who were secular, people who were not Christian, felt slightly alarmed by the idea that he did look to God."[63]

Indeed, such public profession of faith makes some among the citizenry, the clergy, and public officials uncomfortable. Barry Lynn, with Americans United for Separation of Church and State, thinks "Americans want political leaders to have a moral center, but I do not think that Americans expect the President to also be their national pastor."[64] Independent presidential candidate Ralph Nader called Bush "a messianic militarist."[65]

At President Ronald Reagan's funeral, son Ron Reagan chided Bush by comparing the influence of faith upon his father and that of Bush. "Dad was also a deeply, unabashedly religious man. But he never made the fatal mistake of so many politicians—wearing his faith on his sleeve to gain political advantage. True, after he was shot and nearly killed early in his presidency, he came to believe that God had spared him in order that he might do good. But he accepted that as a responsibility, not a mandate. And there is a profound difference."[66]

In essence, many critics of Bush think there should be a clear line drawn between personal faith and public policy. Faith should be a source of inspiration and reflection but not justification for political positions or issues.

During the third presidential debate of 2004, moderator Bob Schieffer asked the most direct and straightforward question as to the role of his faith on policy decisions. "What part does your faith play on your policy decisions?" Bush's response was clear, concise, and straightforward:

> First, my faith plays a lot—a big part in my life. And that's, when I was answering that question, what I was really saying to the person was that I pray a lot. And I do. And my faith is very—it's very personal. I pray for strength. I pray for wisdom. I pray for our troops in harm's way. I pray for my family. I pray for my little girls. But I'm mindful in a free society that people can worship if they want to or not. You're equally an American if you choose to worship an Almighty and if you choose not to. If you're a Christian, Jew or Muslim, you're equally an American. . . . Prayer and religion sustain me. I receive calmness in the storms of the presidency. . . . Religion is an important part. I never want to impose my religion on anybody else. But when I make decisions, I stand on principle, and the principles are derived from who I am.[67]

Thus, throughout the campaign of 2004, there were those who viewed Bush as sincerely guided by principles higher than politics and who welcomed his restoration of values in public life. Others, however, thought Bush was, at best, just hunting for votes and, at worst, displaying moral arrogance.

MORAL VALUES AND THE 2004 PRESIDENTIAL ELECTION

In the immediate afterglow of the 2004 election, reporters and pundits proclaimed that the "religion gap" was the most prominent and fundamental divide in American politics; not the more traditional "gender gap," "party gap," or "age gap."[68] Pollsters found that an individual's level of religious commitment and activity was the primary indicator of voting behavior, certainly more so than education, gender, or income. Social issues such as embryonic stem cell research, gay marriage, abortion, immigration, and a general coarseness of culture provided a context for defining public life and moral values. The various social issues appealed to specific electoral constituencies and became the yardsticks to measure candidate values and personal faith, even in a time of war and international instability.

The relationship between religion and politics reached a new intensity in the 2004 presidential campaign. The personal faith of both candidates and the potential impact upon governing and decision-making became issues throughout the campaigns. Candidates were forced to address issues of faith in speeches, in interviews, and during two of the debates.

In addition, churches toed the line between legally allowed activism and prohibited support for specific candidates. In June 2004, Barry Lynn, executive director of Americans United for the Separation of Church and State, who himself is a United Church minister, observed that the presidential campaign was "the most religiously infused in modern American history."[69] For Steven Waldman, founder and editor of Beliefnet.com, a religious website, this contest generated the most significant effort to motivate religious voters he had ever seen for a presidential campaign.[70] In fact, the politicking became so intense that even the Internal Revenue Service sent letters to both political parties reminding them that churches were not to engage in partisan activities without danger of losing their tax-exempt status.

On Election Day, political observers, pundits, and those in the mainstream media were simply shocked that "moral values" emerged as the most important issue of the election, that church attendance was the best predictor of candidate choice, and that evangelicals turned out in record numbers.

However, there was a series of events that raised "value" issues and concerns for many Americans leading up to the election. Early in the year, the movie *The Passion of the Christ* was released with great fanfare on Ash Wednesday, February 25, 2004. For months it was the number one movie in America. By Election Day, the film had generated $370 million in the United States alone.[71] Throughout the year there were such items as the uproar over Janet Jackson's halftime "wardrobe malfunction" during the Super Bowl, local battles over prayer in schools, posting of the Ten Commandments, challenges to the phrase "Under God" in the Pledge of Allegiance, and, perhaps the greatest stimulus, the one-vote majority ruling of the Massachusetts State Supreme Court in favor of same-sex marriage. Indeed, courts across America, from local up to the Supreme Court of the United States, ignited a renewed "culture war." Although largely unforeseen by members of the media and most political pundits, Bush guru Karl Rove knew how such issues would play in Middle America.

By early summer a *Time* magazine poll made headlines. Americans who considered themselves "very religious" preferred Bush 59 percent to Kerry's 35 percent. In contrast, those who were "not religious" favored Kerry 69 percent to Bush's just 22 percent. When further asked if a president should be guided by his faith when making policy, 63 percent of Democrats said "no," compared to 70 percent of Republicans saying "yes."[72] The "religion gap" continued to be tracked by various news and polling organizations throughout the fall campaign.

Simultaneously, more conservative Christians began to feel targeted and humiliated by members of the media, folks in Hollywood, and various social groups. From a religious perspective, there is a difference between what some refer to as "universalists" and "particularists." Universalists generally believe that all the great religions of the world are equally true and good. Public debate about social issues should be consensus-driven, should be less judgmental, and should display much more tolerance. Particularists, in contrast, do not view all religions as equal. There is right and wrong, good and bad. While universalists portend to rely upon reason, education, and science to back their positions, particularists rely upon scripture and tradition. For example, universalists are more likely to view hot-button issues such as abortion as religious but private and thus not belonging in the public arena. However, particularists view abortion as a moral issue of life. The issue is not one of a scientific debate about when life begins. It is a debate about the social issue of whether human life should be protected.[73]

However, within the last few years, universalists often intimidate, mock, and condescend to particularists. Indiana Republican Congressman Mark Souder best expresses the frustration: "I hope I can clearly communicate that the consensus power structure is so blindly Universalist that they aren't even aware of their behavior. Even the rise of FOX News baffles them. They can't understand that to millions of people, Tom Brokaw, Peter Jennings, and Dan Rather, as well as CNN and other cousins, all espouse a breathtaking uniform Universalist view of the world." He continues, "Conservative Christians, as individuals, do not separate their lives into a private and public sphere. To ask me to check my Christian beliefs at the door is to ask me to expel the Holy Spirit from my life when I serve as a congressman, and that I will not do. Either I am a Christian or I am not; either I reflect His glory or I do not."[74]

A Gallup poll in late October 2004, focusing on moral values and the role of government, found that 71 percent of both Bush supporters and Kerry supporters rated the state of moral values in America as "only fair" or "poor." Although both Bush and Kerry voters agreed as to the moral climate in America, Bush voters were more than twice as likely to believe that government should promote traditional values. Indeed, 75 percent of Bush voters supported the view that government *should promote* traditional values, whereas 64 percent of Kerry voters did not favor government supporting any specific set of social values.[75]

Early on, the Kerry campaign, and mainstream media for that matter, thought the weak economy, job losses, and most certainly the conduct of the war in Iraq would dominate the 2004 election. While conceding the "hard-line conservative right," there was little speculation that religious or moral values would become one of the main issues of the campaign or that Catholics would alter their historic support of Democratic candidates. For Republicans, the evangelical vote and "moral values" were an essential part of their campaign strategy. For Democrats, as the campaign proceeded, discussions of religion, faith, and "moral values" became a distraction and a clear liability for Kerry.

In 2004, Protestants and "other Christians" represented 54 percent of the total vote. Bush received 59 percent of that vote compared to 55 percent in 2000. About 40 percent of Bush's raw vote came from evangelicals. According to Alan Cooperman and Thomas Edsall, Bush won 79 percent of the 26 million evangelical votes.[76] In fact, Bush won every state in which there is significant Southern Baptist presence. White religious conservatives comprised 23 percent of the vote in 2004, but only 14 percent in 2000. This time, Bush got 78 percent of that vote.[77]

Catholics comprised 27 percent of the vote and Bush was the first Republican to receive a majority of the vote at 52 percent, compared to 46 percent in 2000. It is also important to note that Bush got 25 percent of the Jewish vote, up from 19 percent in 2000. Among those for whom a "strong religious faith" was the candidate quality that mattered most, Bush received 91 percent of the vote and 70 percent in terms of the qualities "honesty and trustworthiness."[78]

Interestingly, church attendance was more predictive of voting than religious affiliation. Sixty-four percent of those who attend religious services more than once a week voted for Bush as well as 58 percent of those who attend once a week. The actual vote mirrored many of the polls throughout the fall. Even 50 percent of those who attend religious services a few times a month voted for Bush. Kerry received 54 percent of the vote of those who attend services a few times a year and 62 percent of the vote of those who never attend religious services.[79]

Of course, as already noted, one should not underestimate the vital impact of the gay marriage initiatives on the election results. Tony Perkins, president of the Family Research Council, thinks the same-sex marriage issue was in fact "the hood ornament on the family values wagon that carried the president to a second term."[80] The amendment initiatives to ban same-sex marriage launched petition drives to put the issue to public vote, and those drives resulted in grassroots organizations and voter lists that later were very useful to the Bush campaign. Ultimately, thirteen states approved marriage amendments with eleven on Election Day. In Michigan, the Roman Catholic Church spent $1 million in support of passage of the amendment.[81]

Nearly matching the headlines of the Bush victory was the fact that "moral values" was identified as the most important issue influencing voter choices with 22 percent, topping "economy/jobs" with 20 percent, "terrorism" with 19 percent, and "Iraq" with 15 percent. Based upon the exit poll alternatives of issues offered, there were clear differences in selection between Bush and Kerry voters. Bush received 80 percent of the vote of those who selected "moral values," 86 percent of the vote of those selecting "terrorism," and 57 percent of the vote of those selecting "taxes" as the major issue of influence. In contrast, Kerry received 80 percent of the vote of those selecting "economy/jobs," 77 percent of the vote of those selecting "health care," and 73 percent of the vote of those selecting "Iraq" and "education" as the key issues of influence.[82]

So, just who are "value voters"? James Dobson, chair of the Focus on Family group, defines a "values voter" as someone with "a Christian worldview who begins with the assumption that God is—that he not only exists, but he is the definer of right and wrong, and there are some things that are moral and some things that are immoral, some things that are evil and some things that are good."[83] According to Ralph Reed, "value voters, in the south or the heartland, are concerned about preserving marriage, protecting children from violent or sexually explicit entertainment, teaching the same values in school that are taught at home and reducing the number of teen pregnancies and abortions. More than any single issue, they seek to redress a coarsening of the culture and a loss of civility."[84]

Of course, part of the problem is the way the exit poll question was set up. The question was multiple-choice, forcing a response among the options listed. "Moral values" as just one of the options is broader compared to the other options such as "education," "taxes," "health care," "Iraq," "terrorism," or "economy/jobs." In subsequent discussions and reporting, for some observers, "moral values" included such items as abortion, gay marriage, Hollywood's influence, the general coarsening of American culture, and so forth. For others, it included such concerns as the morality of preemptive war, social justice, poverty, and civil rights, to name just a few. In fact, if one groups the issues in the national exit polls by relevance, war issues ("Iraq and terrorism") results in 34 percent of influence and economic/domestic issues ("economy/jobs," "taxes," and "health care") reflect 33 percent. Thus, any way you view it, 78 percent of respondents chose other options as influencing their vote.

In light of the role "moral values" apparently played in the election, the Gallup organization updated its yearly poll on moral issues usually conducted in May of each year. Post-election, it found that 32 percent think the overall state of moral values in this country is "poor" compared to 40 percent just five months earlier. Equally interesting, 64 percent think the moral values in America are getting "worse" post-election, compared to 77 percent pre-election.[85]

In another post-election poll, the Pew Research Center confirmed that "moral values" led all the other issues in determining the vote by 27 percent. However, when asked what issues influenced their vote as an open-ended question, only 14 percent indicated "moral values." When asked "What comes to mind when you think about 'moral values'?" 44 percent defined the phrase in terms of social issues as abortion (28 percent), homosexuality and gay marriage (29 percent), or stem cell research (4 percent). Twenty-three percent cited personal candidate characteristics as their definition of "moral values."[86]

Bush was asked about the apparent "religious divide" in this country in his first news conference upon reelection. Bush responded,

> The great tradition of America is one where people can worship the way they want to worship. And if they choose not to worship, they're just as patriotic as your neighbor. That is an essential part of why we are a great nation. And I am glad people of faith voted in this election. I am glad—I appreciate all people who voted. . . . And I don't think you ought to read anything into the politics, the moment, about whether or not this nation will become a divided nation over religion. I think the great thing that unites us is the fact you can worship freely if you choose, and if you—you don't have to worship. And if you're a Jew or a Christian or a Muslim, you're equally American. That is such a wonderful aspect of our society. And it is strong today and it'll be strong tomorrow.[87]

In the aftermath of the election, some pundits argued that indeed there is "values gap" between the political parties. Jon Meacham,

Newsweek managing editor, observed that "because the president got his 52 percent, he did talk about the culture of life, he talked about wanting to stand for something amid an ocean of chaos. And more people voted for order than voted for what they thought might be a more chaotic culture under the democrats. . . . I think his agenda is about a tone of moral restoration."[88] Pat Buchanan went one step further. For him, "there's only one leader of the religious right now, one political leader. That's George Bush. . . . The president is the only figure . . . who in his heart has gotten up and said things like Jesus Christ is the philosopher who taught me the most or did the most for me. But what gives him his reach in this community is, he is a man that gets up and says it. Have you heard anyone else since Ronald Reagan used to speak at those evangelical meetings?"[89]

It does appear that Democrats have a problem. Regular churchgoers, pro-lifers, traditionalists are voting Republican in large numbers. Close association of the Democratic Party with secularists is problematic, especially when over 90 percent of Americans say they believe in God and nearly 70 percent belong to some church.[90] Recall that Bush took the majority vote among Orthodox Jews, Catholics, and married women. He also made significant gains in the Hispanic vote, although marginally among African-Americans. All these groups traditionally support the Democratic Party.

In the end, Kerry lacked fairly basic credibility when trying to appeal to voters on "religious values." In debates and on the stump, he talked of how his faith informs his views on poverty, the environment, social justice. But then he declares he can't follow his faith on issues of abortion, for which church views are very clear. The obvious problematic issue for many people of faith is that if one believes something as true, one has an obligation to act on that truth, or simply be hypocritical. In short, Kerry wanted it both ways, to claim he was guided by faith on some issues and not others. It was simply viewed by many as a political and theological dodge.

Another perspective offered was that many voted for Bush in 2004, not because of what he might do in terms of social issues, but because of the kind of person he is in terms of integrity, honesty, and trustworthiness. Michael Gerson, Bush speechwriter and policy advisor, notes that Bush is an "incrementalist" and will not make wholesale social changes. While Bush believes that every human life should be welcomed and legally protected, he also believes that social consensus must exist before social change. "Neither Bush's personality nor his ideology meshes with the profile of dogmatic social engineer." Gerson thinks Bush's invocations of God are never gratuitous but are appropriate to the context of events—a funeral, a prayer breakfast, a national morning State of the Union address, and so forth.[91]

Of course, there were academics and pundits who did not think religion or "moral values" were the determining factors in the campaign. Actually, moderates, not the religious right, defeated John Kerry. For example, 38 percent of those who think abortion should be legal in most cases voted for Bush. So did 22 percent of those who favor same-sex marriage and 52 percent of those who favor civil unions. Even a third of those who do not favor government action to solve social problems voted for Bush. Exit polls found that 10 percent of those who voted for Gore in 2000 voted for Bush in 2004.[92]

Pollster Andrew Kohut, director of the Pew Research Center for the People and the Press, thinks the importance of religion in the Bush victory was indeed well overstated. For him, turnout was the decisive factor in the Bush victory. There were simply more Republicans, both more "religious" and "less religious," who voted. Ultimately, Kohut thinks Republicans were successful in turning the election into a referendum on Bush instead of one on Kerry. In the end, voters "went for a more straight-talking, tougher-sounding candidate, and while moral issues and religion played the important role it typically does, I don't believe it was the decisive role."[93]

Barry Burden concurs and argues that Bush won because married and white women increased their support for the Republican ticket. In fact, "simply put, Bush won the 2004 presidential election because he improved his share of the vote in a wide range of states."[94] Thus, evangelicals turned out at a higher rate, as did every other demographic group. Burden thinks that white women, who are evenly distributed across all the states, are responsible for almost all of Bush's increase between the two elections.

CONCLUSION

Over a hundred years ago, British writer G. K. Chesterton described America as "a nation with the soul of a church." Indeed, according to a Pew Forum poll just weeks before the 2004 election, seven in ten Americans indicated they wanted a presidential candidate to have strong religious beliefs.[95]

Of course, there is a rich history of American presidents evoking the name of God. George Washington, in signing the first Thanksgiving proclamation, decreed that November 26 "be devoted by the people of these States to the service of that great and glorious Being who is the beneficent author of all the good that was, that is, or that will be; that we may then all unite in rendering unto Him our sincere and humble thanks for His kind care and protection of the people of this country previous to their becoming a nation." In his Farewell Address, Washington proclaimed that of all the "dispositions" that lead to political prosperity, morality above all is the most indispensable, that "both reason and experience forbid us to expect that national morality can prevail in exclusion of religious principle."[96]

The fathers of our nation and signers of the Declaration of Independence added the words that men "are endowed by their Creator with certain unalienable rights." As early as 1774, Thomas Jefferson wrote, "The God who gave us life, gave us liberty at the same time."[97] While there is some debate just how religious the forefathers were in today's context, there is no doubt they evoked God's name and called for His blessings upon our young nation and its endeavors.

During the Civil War, it was Congress with Lincoln's support that put the words "In God We Trust" on the nation's coins. During the Cold War, Congress put those words in the Pledge of Allegiance in 1954 and on paper currency in 1955. Just a year later, those same words became the official motto of the United States of America.[98]

By the era of the 1950s, "the tradition started by Jefferson, and perfected by Lincoln, was firmly established: It was a tradition of American Presidents who, regardless of the relative strength of their private faith, freely employed the rhetorical imagery of the Bible, generally the New Testament, in invoking God's aid and blessing for the nation—but not in a way that chose sides among denominations—or among Americans themselves."[99]

From a historical perspective, social and value issues have always dominated American politics. During the years of the Great Depression and the New Deal, electoral success focused more on economic issues. However, since the 1960s, social issues and values have increased in importance in American politics.

Prior to 1972, there was no religion gap. Those who regularly attended church voted the same as those who did not. However, Nixon appealed to the traditionalists, the "silent majority," resulting in the emerging gap between the parties. From 1972 until 1992, the religion gap between the parties stayed in the single digit. However, during Clinton's second term, the gap widened between the parties. During the 2000 presidential campaign, Bush emphasized the role of religion in his personal life and pledged to uphold moral values in the Oval Office. Throughout his first term, the religion gap grew between the parties. The only exception is with African-Americans, who have become the most supporting constituency group for the Democratic Party. In the past, Catholics were a dependable Democratic constituency; today they are a swing-voting block.

Although several years old, the religious identification survey by the Graduate Center at CUNY found that 77 percent of Americans classify themselves as Christian. Only about 8 million identify themselves as non-Christians.[100] Those who call themselves Evangelical Christians have increased from 22 percent in 1960 to 34 percent today.[101] According to a Gallup poll in June 2004, about six in ten Americans said religion was a "very important" part of their lives and believe religion can answer all or most of today's societal problems. In addition, a majority of Americans indicated that they attend religious services at least once a month, a third indicated that they attend every week, and six in ten belong to some church or synagogue. Less than one in ten Americans have no religious affiliation at all.[102]

Thus, American presidents since George Washington have included religious language and references to God in public discourse. Claims of the United States as "divinely chosen nation" with requests for God's blessings have been commonplace. Such discourse reflects the "civil religion" in which leaders emphasize religious symbols and transcendent principles to engender a sense of unity and shared identity. We can ill afford to purge the public sphere of religious or value discourse. Indeed, it is the commonalities of our attitudes, beliefs, and values that unite and bind us given our diversities of race, income, and geography.

So, what about George W. Bush? As a human being and as a leader, George W. Bush is a person of character, faith, integrity, and discipline. One certainly may disagree with him on issues and policy, but one certainly knows where he stands, what he favors, and the direction he wishes to take the nation. It is that sense of values and grounding that enabled him to lead the nation post-9/11 and to wage the war on terrorism.

I personally take comfort in the fact that Bush *is* a man of faith. It doesn't make him always right or perfect, far from it. But his faith establishes a clear set of values and modes of conduct as an individual and as a public leader. These values are clearly expressed in his public discourse and private behavior. Actually, the sense of values makes him more predictable. He understands that he must be a role model and expresses regret of his "youthful" indiscretions and their potential impact upon younger Americans. From all accounts, the public Bush is the same as the private Bush. He does not separate the public sphere from the private sphere.

I do understand those who disagree with Bush on domestic and foreign policy and issues. I even understand those who have concerns about his management style and worldviews. However, I do not understand the apparent "hatred" of Bush by some *because* of his faith or *because* of his public profession of faith. In terms of the basic principles of leadership,

George W. Bush is a welcome change from William Jefferson Clinton. And, in 2004, Bush was clearly preferred over John Kerry, especially when comparing the personal leadership qualities of both men as reflected in exit polls.

Finally, George W. Bush understands the uniqueness of America and the interrelationships among our private and public values as they relate to a successful democracy. In his second inaugural address, Bush reiterated a theme heard during his campaign and in the debates. It is also the theme or philosophy of this book. Freedom is a gift from God and requires individual integrity and character if the society is to be democratic, fair, and just.

> From the day of our founding, we have proclaimed that every man and woman on this earth has rights and dignity and matchless values because they bear the image of the maker of heaven and earth. Across generations, we have proclaimed the imperative of self-government, because no one is fit to be a master, and no one deserves to be a slave. . . . In America's ideal of freedom, the public interest depends on private character, on integrity and tolerance toward others and the rule of conscience in our own lives. . . . That edifice of character is built in families, supported by communities with standards, and sustained in our national life by the truths of Sinai, the Sermon on the Mount, the words of the Koran and the varied faiths of our people. . . . We go forward with complete confidence in the eventual triumph of freedom. Not because history runs on the wheels of inevitability; it is human choices that move events. Not because we consider ourselves a chosen nation; God moves and chooses as He wills. We have confidence because freedom is the permanent hope of mankind, the hunger in dark places, the longing of the soul.[103]

NOTES

1. Robert Shogan, *Bad News: Where the Press Goes Wrong in the Making of the President* (Chicago: Ivan R. Dee, 2001), 199–200.
2. T. Nickens, "Bush Acknowledges DUI Conviction in '76," *St. Petersburg Times*, November 3, 2000, A1.
3. D. Balz, "Bush Acknowledges 1976 DUI Arrest," *Washington Post*, November 3, 2000, A1; A. Cohen, "Fallout from a Midnight Ride: An Old Arrest for Driving under the Influence Revives the Issue of Bush's 'Irresponsible Youth,'" *Time*, November 13, 2000, 43; G. Lardner, "Bush Avoided Earlier Queries on DUI Charge," *Washington Post*, November 4, 2000, A15.
4. Bush won six states by a narrow margin: Missouri (51/47), Nevada (49/46), New Hampshire (48/47), Oregon (by just 540 votes), Tennessee

(51/48), and Louisiana (53/45). Likewise, Gore won by a narrow margin in Iowa (49/48), Minnesota (48/46), New Mexico (by 346 votes), and Wisconsin (by 396 votes).

5. Lardner, "Bush Avoided Earlier Queries on DUI Charge," A15.
6. Cohen, "Fallout from a Midnight Ride," A1.
7. Lardner, "Bush Avoided Earlier Queries on DUI Charge," A15.
8. Lardner, "Bush Avoided Earlier Queries on DUI Charge," A15.
9. Shogan, *Bad News*, 220–21.
10. M. Allen and D. Balz, "Bush Seeks to Minimize DUI Fallout; Candidate Says He's Learned to Lead from Past 'Mistake,'" *Washington Post*, November 4, 2000, A1.
11. All quotes from Bush's statement and interaction with the media are from *CNN.Com Transcripts*, http://www.cnn.com/TRANSCRIPTS/0011/02/se.08.html, retrieved May 29, 2003.
12. M. Kerbel, "The Media: Old Frames in a Time of Transition," in *The Election of 2000*, M. Nelson, ed. (Washington, DC: Congressional Quarterly Press, 2001), 126.
13. James Ceasar and Andrew Busch, *The Perfect Tie* (Lanham, MD: Rowman & Littlefield, 2001), 153.
14. Nickens, "Bush Acknowledges DUI Conviction," A1.
15. D. Wilkie, "Bush DUI Turns into Firestorm: Arrest That He Kept from Public Becomes the News of the Hour," *The San Diego Union-Tribune*, November 4, 2000, A1.
16. P. Nicholas and D. Goldstein, "Bush Struggles to Keep the Focus on Issues; He Blames Timing of Drunken-Driving Report on 'Dirty Politics,'" *Milwaukee Journal Sentinel*, November 4, 2000, A1.
17. M. Hershey, "The Campaign and the Media," in *The Election of 2000*, Gerald Pomper, ed. (New York: Chatham House, 2001), 65.
18. Ceasar and Busch, *The Perfect Tie*, 153; F. Newport, "Most Voters Say That Bush DUI Incident Will Have No Effect on Vote," *Gallup*, http://www.gallup.com/poll/releases/pr001105.asp, retrieved May 15, 2003; E. Walsh, "Campaign 2000: Costliest Race Nears End; Bush, Gore Running Close; Candidates Seek to Lift Turnout in Key States," *Washington Post*, November 6, 2000, A1.
19. *USA Today*.
20. M. Barabak, "Campaign 2000: Bush's 1976 Arrest in Maine Is Revealed," *Los Angeles Times*, November 3, 2000, A28.
21. Hank Kenski, B. Aylor, and Kate Kenski, "Explaining the Vote in a Divided Country: The Presidential Election of 2000," in *The 2000 Presidential Campaign: A Communication Perspective*, Robert E. Denton, Jr., ed. (Westport, CT: Praeger, 2002), 255.
22. Kenski, Aylor, and Kenski, "Explaining the Vote in a Divided Country," 258.
23. PollingReport.com, http://www.pollingreport.com/2000.htm, retrieved July 24, 2004.

24. Gary Jacobson, "The Bush Presidency and the American Electorate," in *The George W. Bush Presidency,* Fred Greenstein, ed. (Baltimore: Johns Hopkins University Press, 2003), 198.

25. James Pfiffner, "Introduction: Assessing the Bush Presidency," in *Considering the Bush Presidency,* Gary Gregg and Mark Rozell, eds. (New York: Oxford University Press, 2004), 1.

26. John Podhoretz, *Bush Country* (New York: St. Martin's Press, 2004), 74.

27. Evan Thomas, Tamara Lipper, and Rebecca Sinderbrand, "The Road to Resolve," *Newsweek,* September 6, 2002, 32.

28. Ronald Kessler, *A Matter of Character* (New York: Sentinel, 2004), 6–7.

29. Michael Dimock, "Bush and Public Opinion," in *Considering the Bush Presidency,* Gary Gregg and Mark Rozell, eds. (New York: Oxford University Press, 2004), 74.

30. Hugh Heclo, "The Political Ethos of George W. Bush," in *The George W. Bush Presidency,* Fred Greenstein, ed. (Baltimore: Johns Hopkins University Press, 2003), 20.

31. John Dilulio, "A View from Within," in *The George W. Bush Presidency,* Fred Greenstein, ed. (Baltimore: Johns Hopkins University Press, 2003), 248.

32. Kessler, *A Matter of Character,* 34.

33. Podhoretz, *Bush Country,* 6.

34. Kessler, *A Matter of Character,* 129.

35. Thomas, Lipper, and Sinderbrand, "The Road to Resolve," 36.

36. Carolyn Thompson and James Ware, *The Leadership Genius of George W. Bush* (Hoboken, NJ: John Wiley & Sons, 2003), 31.

37. Kessler, *A Matter of Character,* 87–88.

38. Kessler, *A Matter of Character,* 9.

39. Kessler, *A Matter of Character,* 1.

40. Kessler, *A Matter of Character,* 2 and 109.

41. Kessler, *A Matter of Character,* 72.

42. Kessler, *A Matter of Character,* 11–12.

43. George W. Bush, "Address by George W. Bush, President of the United States, Delivered to the Nation, Washington, D.C., September 11, 2001," *Vital Speeches of the Day,* LXVII, 738.

44. George W. Bush, "Address by George W. Bush, President of the United States, Delivered to a Joint Session of Congress and the American People, Washington, D.C., September 20, 2001," *Vital Speeches of the Day,* LXVII, 760.

45. Bush, "Address by George W. Bush, September 20, 2001," 761.

46. Andrew Glass, "The War on Terrorism Goes Online," Working Paper Series #2002-3, (Cambridge, MA: Shorenstein Center on the Press, Politics and Public Policy, 2002), 4.

47. Pfiffner, "Introduction: Assessing the Bush Presidency," 5.

48. Dimock, "Bush and Public Opinion," 78.

49. Dimock, "Bush and Public Opinion," 82.

50. Podhoretz, *Bush Country,* 78.

51. Podhoretz, *Bush Country,* 30.

52. Podhoretz, *Bush Country*, 11.
53. Podhoretz, *Bush Country*, 19.
54. Podhoretz, *Bush Country*, 220.
55. Carl Cannon, "Bush and God," *National Journal*, January 3, 2004, 17.
56. Jacobson, "The Bush Presidency," 199.
57. Jacobson, "The Bush Presidency," 227.
58. Much of the information in this section and an extended analysis can be found in "Religion, Evangelicals and 'Moral Issues' in the 2004 Presidential Campaign," by Robert E. Denton, Jr., in *The 2004 Presidential Campaign: A Communication Perspective*, Robert E. Denton, Jr., ed. (Lanham, MD: Rowman & Littlefield, 2005), 255–81.
59. Guy Lawson, "George W.'s Personal Jesus," *Gentlemen's Quarterly*, September 2003, 332.
60. Arnold Hamilton, "Wooing Catholics a Key to Winning Presidential Election," *The Dallas Morning News*, April 14, 2004, http://www.dallas news.com, retrieved September 9, 2004.
61. Lawson, "George W.'s Personal Jesus," 396.
62. Fox News Channel, *The O'Reilly Factor*, April 29, 2004, http://web.lexisnexis .com/universe/document?_m=75ef21fcbd07b65b2e4be838cc03d7&_docnum-1&wchp=dGLbV1b&_md5=6cdf2d7fb1261, retrieved September 30, 2004.
63. Fox News Channel, *The O'Reilly Factor*, April 29, 2004.
64. Nancy Gibbs, "The Faith Factor," *Time*, June 21, 2004, 33.
65. William Schneider, "Bush's Father Figure," *National Journal*, May 1, 2004, 1372.
66. Scott Shepard, "The Book of Votes," *Atlanta Journal-Constitution*, May 1, 2004, B1.
67. "Transcript: Third Presidential Debate," Washingtonpost.com, October 13, 2004, http://www.washingtonpost.com/wp-srv/politics/debatereferee/debate_1013.html, retrieved November 14, 2004.
68. See note 58.
69. "Whose Side Is God On This Time?" *The Toronto Star*, June, 20 2004, http://web.lexisnexis.com/universe/document?_m=b262b1765e345f0026 7cfa7c70eca718&_docnum=19&wchp=dGLbVzb-zSkVA&_md 5=9b1646145ab, retrieved August 31, 2004.
70. Carol Eisenberg, "God & Politics," *Newsday*, September 1, 2004, http://web.lexis-nexis.com/universe/document?_m=dca56e9b4171fa779fdb 1a9e6&_docnum=105&wchp=dGLbVzz-zSkVA&_md5=ea236f2c9aa35f69e 765397916ccadf, retrieved September 9, 2004.
71. Borys Kit, "Hot-Button Movies Iced for Top Golden Globe," *Toronto Star*, November 11, 2004, A27.
72. Gibbs, "The Faith Factor," 26–28.
73. "One Electorate Under God? A Dialogue on Religion and American Politics," July 21, 2004, http://pewforum.org/events/print.php? EventID=59, retrieved August 31, 2004.
74. "One Electorate Under God?"

75. "Bush Voters Support Active Government Role in Values Arena," Gallup Poll News Service, November 29, 2004, http://www.gallup.com/poll/content/print.aspx?ci=14158, retrieved December 3, 2004.

76. Alan Cooperman and Thomas Edsall, "Evangelicals Say They Led Charge for the GOP," WashingtonPost.com, November 8, 2004, http://www.washingtonpost.com/ac2/wp-dyn/A32793-2004Nov7?language=printer, retrieved November 8, 2004.

77. "National Exit Poll Results," *AP Politics*, November 2, 2004, http://politics.ap.org/eln2004_genexitpolls/p_us.shtml, retrieved November 3, 2004; Linda Feidmann, "How Lines of the Culture War Have Been Redrawn," *Christian Science Monitor*, November 15, 2004, http://web.lexisnexis.com/universe/document?_m=3b674486b262172d5237ad2d9fe03cbd&_docnum=6&wchp=dGLbVzz-zSkVA&_md5=07cda742656, retrieved November 16, 2004; Ralph Reed, "So Who Were Those Value Voters?" *USA Today*, December 5, 2004, http://www.usatoday.com/news/opinion/editorials/2004-12-05-values-reed_x.htm, retrieved December 6, 2004; Henry Kenski, "Explaining the Vote in a Divided Country: The Presidential Election of 2000," in Robert E. Denton, Jr., ed., *The 2000 Presidential Campaign: A Communication Perspective* (Westport, CT: Praeger, 2002), 240–41.

78. "National Exit Poll Results."

79. "National Exit Poll Results."

80. Cooperman and Edsall, "Evangelicals Say They Led Charge."

81. Cooperman and Edsall, "Evangelicals Say They Led Charge."

82. "Bush Voters Support Active Government Role in Values Arena."

83. Cooperman and Edsall, "Evangelicals Say They Led Charge."

84. Reed, "So Who Were Those Value Voters?"

85. "Moral Issues," Gallup Poll News Service, http://www.gallup.com/poll/content/print.aspx?ci=1681, retrieved December 3, 2004.

86. "Voters Liked Campaign 2004, But Too Much 'Mud-Slinging,'" The Pew Research Center, November 11, 2004, http://people-press.org/reports/display.php3?ReportID=233, November 14, 2004.

87. "Text of Bush News Conference, First after Re-election," Associated Press, November 4, 2004, http://politics.ap.org/Gov2004_whu/bushnewsconf_110404.shtml, retrieved November 9, 2004.

88. "Hardball with Chris Matthews for Nov. 19," MSNBC.com, November 19, 2004, http://www.msnbc.msn.com/id/6557177/print/1/displaymode/1098, retrieved November 22, 2004.

89. "Hardball with Chris Matthews for Nov. 19."

90. Gibbs, "The Faith Factor," 29.

91. Kathleen Parker, "President Doesn't Use Faith as a Bargaining Tool," *Gwinnett Daily Post Online*, December 13, 2004, http://gwinnettdailyonline.com/GDP/archive/article4B1054F1E3404954A473E0DD1C84KB01.asp?printerFriendly=true, retrieved December 13, 2004.

92. "National Exit Poll Results."
93. "Press Briefing, How the Faithful Voted: Political Alignments & the Religious Divide in Election 2004," Pew Research Center for the People and the Press, November 17, 2004, http://www.people-press.org, retrieved November 17, 2004.
94. Barry Burden, "An Alternative Account of the 2004 Presidential Election," *The Forum*, 2 (4), http://www.bepress.com/forum/vol2/iss4/art2, retrieved January 4, 2005.
95. Eisenberg, "God & Politics."
96. Cannon, "Bush and God,"14.
97. Cannon, "Bush and God,"14.
98. Cannon, "Bush and God,"14.
99. Cannon, "Bush and God,"14.
100. "American Religious Identification Survey," The Graduate Center (CUNY), 2001, http://www.gc.cuny.edu/studies/key_findings.htm, retrieved September 13, 2004.
101. Eisenberg, "God & Politics."
102. "Religion," Gallup Poll News Service, June 6, 2004, http://www.gallup .com/poll/content/default.aspx?ci+1690, retrieved June 7, 2004.
103. "There Is No Justice Without Freedom," Washingtonpost.com, January 21, 2005, http://www.washingtonpost.com/ac2/wp-dyn/A23747-2005Jn20? language=printer, retrieved January 21, 2005.

The Presidency, Moral Leadership, and a Government as Good as the American People

Why not the best?

—JIMMY CARTER

To speak of reform or change of the American presidency without recognizing the public's perceptions, attitudes, and beliefs about the nature of the office is clearly doomed to failure. Since the founding of the nation, Americans have nearly always favored solving problems by reforming structures. However, in this case, the problem lies not with the institution per se but with some occupants of the office and citizen criteria for election. Thus, for me, the contemporary problems of the presidency go beyond constitutional-legalistic questions, institutional organizational charts, pressures of economic elites or interest groups, or the "real" personality of individual presidents. The concern is grounded in our failure to recognize the importance of the historic values or role of the office, as well as our failure as citizens to elect only the best to serve.

Some would argue that if there is a problem with the institutional presidency, it is the gap between the symbolic, mythic, historical presidential persona and the harsh "realities" and "demands" of today's world. The nation's mythic, symbolic expectations of the office are no longer apropos to meet the challenges of the twenty-first century. Even some of the classic works on the presidency that highly praised the institution subtly forewarned of impending danger. Clinton Rossiter's 1956 classic "white knight" orientation to the presidency proclaims, at the beginning of the section on the future of the office, "we need no special gift of prophecy to predict a long and exciting future for the American Presidency."[1] Yet later he acknowledges that "perhaps the softest spot of all in the general health of the Presidency lies in the gap between the responsibility and authority, between promise and performance, in the areas of public administration."[2] Indeed, modern presidents have proclaimed wars on inflation, poverty, crime, urban decay, pollution, hunger, and cancer, to name just a few. Yet the battles are continually lost and the wars are soon abandoned or forgotten. As a result, Americans are becoming accustomed to presidential promises that go largely unfulfilled.

Others would claim that my very concern about the historic dimensions of the presidency would only feed additional cynicism and concern. Today nearly all aspects of our life are subject to the manipulation of images. Consequently, this has resulted in the blurring of knowledge, desires, and expectations. National politics have largely become a game of illusion mistaken for reality, competition for images rather than ideals. A successful president, many would argue, must become even more concerned with images than issues, for today, issues are used primarily in terms of projecting the correct image, to attract key constituencies and as a reflection of genuine concern. The gap between expectations and what can actually be achieved inevitably mars presidential credibility and makes the modern presidency vulnerable.

All presidents since Franklin Roosevelt have discovered and openly acknowledge that the gap between what they want to do when elected and what they can do once in office is enormous. This is not to argue simplistically that all presidents or presidential candidates are liars or incompetent. Rather, it emphasizes the distinction between winning an election and governing the nation. The former is a process of highly planned, abstract appeals, historically successful yet disconnected from the daily pragmatics of governing.

The difficulty of the American presidency equally lies within the public's conception of the institution. There are three major factors that have contributed significantly to the formation of today's managerial view of the office. First, previous administrations have left legacies of presidential conduct and behavior that have contributed to the formation of expectations of specific behavior, real or perceived. The legacies of presidents of the second half of the twentieth century have been less than sterling. As public leadership becomes more challenging, our leaders have become more disappointing.

The second major factor is the role of mass media. The mass media, especially television, favors images over substance and ideas. Historically, heroes have always been respected and honored in our nation. Today, however, we have replaced hero worship with celebrity worship. By confusing the two, according to Daniel Boorstin, the nation deprives itself of good role models and comes to believe that people are great because they are famous instead of that people are famous because they are great.[3] Genuine heroes are distinguished by achievement gaining recognition over a long period of time—usually at least a generation. In contrast, laments Boorstin, the celebrity is distinguished by his or her image and created by the media. The celebrity is always contemporary and survives by gossip, public opinion, magazines, newspapers, and television.

As celebrities, people are "known for their well-knownness."[4] The mediated conversations of presidents with the public provide a false intimacy because they do not reveal the true back regions of presidents' thoughts or ideas. The illusion is one of spontaneity and accessibility.[5] In Clinton's case, Joe Klein noted that "there is a facile opacity to this style of leadership: even though we get to hear about his 12-step program, his stepfather's alcoholism, his mother's cancer, his brother's drug addiction, the host himself remains elusive, a kaleidoscope of comforting images."[6] We participate vicariously in their life through "artificial interactions." At best, according to Roderick Hart, "television gives us a one-dimensional presidency."[7] Technology is at the heart of our transition into an information society. Continued advances in computers and telecommunications are leading into a convergence of traditional mass media. In fact, all communications technologies are converging into a common computer-readable or digital form. Many observers speculate that the introduction of digital television will be the key event in placing a computer processor in virtually every home. And when computers enter our homes, mass media consumption patterns change. Mass media convergence influences the way we work, form social relationships, form new identities, and develop new cultures.[8]

Today, it is only through the media that we come to know our leaders. And with the frequency of appearance we feel that we have come to know our presidents intimately. It is virtually impossible to distinguish between our political system and the media as separate entities.

Kathleen Jamieson argues that the interpersonal, intimate context created through television requires a "new eloquence," one in which candidates and presidents adopt a personal and revealing style that engages the audience in conversation.[9] Presidents who increasingly rely on the medium of television are forced into playing the communication game by television's rules. This not only means shorter speeches, it also means speeches that are crafted specifically for television. Presidential speech is increasingly familiar, personalized, and self-revealing. The "presumption of intimacy" attempts to make the audience feel as if they know the president as a dear friend and to force the audience to render positive, personal judgments. Frequent "conversations" lead to friendship, trust, and intimacy with the nation. Issue disagreements are less important and tolerated because of the appearance of friendship.[10]

Political scholars, journalists, and pundits raise concerns about the new presidential "public address." Mediated presidential conversation fails to properly inform and educate the public on political matters. Mediated presidential discourse encourages citizens' continued emphasis on persona, likability, rather than on substance of policy.[11] As the public becomes even more reliant upon television as a source of political information, the medium increasingly simplifies the information and, consequently, the abilities to recognize, perform, and appreciate complex social issues also decline. Franko Ferrarotti observes that "as we are informed, we know everything about everything, but we no longer understand anything. It is purely cerebral information that does not manage to touch the deeper levels of human beings."[12] For Roderick Hart, "television miseducates the citizenry but, worse, it makes that miseducation attractive."[13] In reality, the public does not know what they think they know and the public does not care about what they do not know.

Perhaps the most damaging aspect of all mediated conversations is the public's open acknowledgment that all political talk is performance. Martin Schram argues that the public's recognition that all presidents are ultimately "acting" merely leads to acceptance of the ability to perform as the essential qualification for office: "The quest for personal leadership becomes a self-destructive quest in which all pretenders are found to be just that. In the end, the grammar of electronic electioneering teaches people to be content with their inability to find a 'real leader' and to be comfortable with elected officials who are comfortable faking it."[14] Indeed, Joseph Cappella and Kathleen Jamieson link the rising level of voter cynicism and the nature of media coverage of political events and issues.[15] They argue that "both the contemporary journalistic culture and a focus on strategy, conflict, and motives invite cynicism."[16] Finally, mediated conversations with politicians and leaders also create a short-term political environment. The focus is on the person, not the issue; the momentary emotion, not the long-term commitment; the immediate image, not the long-term solution. Through the conversations, presidents engender trust and identification rather than the process of rational decision-making. There is, as Jamieson notes, a continual divorce between speech and thought, character and ideas.[17] And in the twenty-first century, there will be communication technologies unknown today that will further impact the very nature of presidential discourse and public interactions.

CHALLENGES FOR THE
INSTITUTIONAL PRESIDENCY

The world has certainly changed dramatically in the last fifty years. The size, power, and prestige of the office have grown. Yet there are major challenges to the very power and scope of the office to provide genuine leadership. First is the challenge of the nature of audience. Of course, all effective communication is audience centered. However, the dilemma for presidents is, who is the audience? Congress? Opinion elites? Citizens? Party regulars? The bureaucracy? The world or international community?

The difficulty is that specific messages, depending upon the audience, can appear contradictory or may alienate some listeners. An aggressive legislative agenda may well be received very differently by citizens at large, the established bureaucracy, or party regulars. As an example, think of Clinton's gays-in-the-military policy of "don't ask, don't tell." It mobilized the opposition, cut short his presidential "honeymoon" period, alienated the military establishment, initially thrilled a core constituent group, but puzzled the general public. The same complications were true of the health care debate of 1994 and will be true for pending future discussions by the Bush administration on Social Security, genuine tax reform, and Medicare funding, to name just a few.

Traditionally, communication is thought to be the primary means through which a nation forges a common identity, a common purpose, and a common resolve. However, it is becoming more difficult to provide a unified message to many different audiences simultaneously.

An irony of the explosion of communication technologies is the shift by mass media toward smaller and smaller target audiences. "Narrowcasting" instead of "broadcasting" is now the norm. Narrowcasting directs media channels to specific segments of the audience. One downside of the new information society is social fragmentation. Social groups communicate among members and become better able to customize culture for their own interests to the exclusion of others. Joseph Straubhaar and Robert LaRose caution, "With less and less shared information, culture fragments and nation-states could dissolve in chaos. At some point, we would no longer be a nation of Americans, or even of Anglo, African, Asian, or Hispanic Americans, but a disjointed collection of cults and splinter groups."[18]

From a political perspective, special interest groups utilize the latest communication strategies and techniques to activate their constituencies. As the public becomes more fragmented, it loses its social coherence. For Peter Dahlgren, the public "becomes reduced to a group of spectators whose acclaim is to be periodically mobilized, but whose intrusion in fundamental political questions is to be minimized."[19] In terms of the presidential discourse, audiences have become too numerous, too diverse, and too political. Indeed, according to Bruce Gronbeck, the modern electronic media and our pursuit of the democratic ideal have produced a fragmented and splintered society.[20] As citizens, we are separated from each other by many demographic, psychographic, ideological, and thematic variables that allow presidents and politicians to appeal to us around specific clusters of beliefs, attitudes, and values. The more we divide audiences, the less potential for unity and appeal to commonplaces.

The second challenge, globalization, is related to that of audience, but magnifies the dilemma. Globalization is a reality in numerous areas ranging from economics to politics, from media programs to culture. Our peace and prosperity is a matter of world peace and prosperity. Our peace and security now depend upon the security of faraway places and peoples whose histories and issues may go back thousands of years. From a technological perspective, to travel the world is no longer a matter of years, months, or days, but mere seconds.

The traditional distinction between domestic and foreign policy is less informative. Price supports, minimum wage, or tariff policies, to name a few, not only have domestic implications but also may impact relations with other nations. Think of our numerous challenges concerning China. Should we expand trade with China? Should we grant them "Most Favored Nation" status? Should they become part of the already controversial World Trade Organization? What should the role of civil rights play in market, trade, and economic considerations?

World events control us more than we are able to control world events. As we witnessed in late 1998, from an economic perspective, when Japan sneezes, we catch a cold. As our interventions in Bosnia and Kosovo, like other police actions and, of course, our war on terrorism against Afghanistan and Iraq post-9/11, demonstrate, it is becoming more difficult and almost impossible to avoid some role in international conflicts. Somewhat ironically, presidential attempts to reinvigorate national pride and historical prestige enhance internationally the very atmosphere that makes future conflicts even more likely. Just twenty years ago there was great discussion about the "Americanization" of media in the world. Today, it is "globalization."

The third challenge to the institutional presidency is one of persuasion. As society and technology change, so do the ways presidents campaign and govern. For much of our history, public oratory provided the main avenue to success and popular esteem. Politicians were expected to frequently make long public orations. The famous "soapbox" or "stump" campaigns were deliberative in nature. Politicians articulated elements of political philosophy. Political oratory was an instrument for conducting national business and a means of public education, and served as an end in itself—a mode of creative expression.

Jürgen Habermas talks about the "transformation of the public sphere" into a classical and a modern period.[21] In the classical period, public debate was diverse, robust, eloquent, reasoned, and vigorous. An example would be the classic Lincoln-Douglas series of debates of 1858. The modern period is one of decline. Peter Dahlgren argues that "with mass democracy, the public loses its exclusivity; its socio-discursive coherence comes apart as many less educated citizens enter the scene. . . . The boundaries between public and private, both in political economic terms and in cultural terms, begin to dissipate."[22]

Today, presidents spend more and more time attempting to influence public opinion concerning their policies as well as their personal popularity as a strategy to maximize influence with members of Congress. Samuel Kernell recognized the growing trend and detailed the strategy of "going public" by presidents to promote themselves as well as policies in Washington by appealing directly to the American public for support.[23] "Presidents have created both individual and institutional responses to the pressures of attempting to control much that is uncontrollable. In response to this pressure, individual presidents give an increasing number of speeches that reflect ever more ceremonial, abstract content."[24] Indeed, presidential scholar George Edwards recently acknowledged that the primary task of presidents is to "build supportive coalitions" rather than change public opinion.[25]

Today, it is nearly impossible for a president to have enough time, access, or repetition of message to persuade citizens of anything in the traditional way of thinking about persuasion. At the very least, today the predominant mode of proof is pathos or emotion. Presidential discourse is more about reinforcement and maintaining the "market share" of key constituent groups than engaging in a genuine dialogue. Even in times of crisis, presidential persuasion is "short-term." Oppositional views are aired immediately and given credence by the media. Today, the news cycle is no longer twenty-four hours, but a matter of minutes. The lack of the possibility of presidential persuasion in the classical sense means a constant state of administrative spin, advocacy, polarization, and the use of surrogates.

With these challenges in mind, the presidency of the twenty-first century is a very different creature. Audience appeals and identification are more important than argument. Narrative and drama are more important than reason and evidence. To appeal and to build public coalitions, presidents tell stories, provide anecdotes, involve the audience, and reference historical myths.

With the transformation of presidential discourse in both form and content comes also the change of the nature of political authority. Citizens are less deferential to traditional sources and claims of authority. Performance and competence are more important than ideas or promises. Citizens judge the legitimacy of state leaders by management competencies rather than some moral or spiritual standards. A competitive global economy focuses attention on the bottom line rather than some moral authority or challenge. As already noted several times, many political observers argue that President Clinton's survival of the impeachment challenge resulted in the public's distinction between his public and private behavior.

The new presidential discourse responds to very different citizen needs, perceptions, and relations to political authority. "Narrative truth" is very different from "moral argument." Common sense reigns supreme. As William Lewis recognized more than a decade ago, "the story is the primary basis for defining the situation, morality is the primary basis for justifying public policy, and common sense is the primary basis for analyzing political issues."[26]

Ronald Collins and David Skover fear the "death of discourse" in America. They view an irony of "discourse dying in America, yet everywhere free speech thrives."[27] For them, discourse is interaction characterized by reason and by method, and with purpose. It is not "trivial talk." Discourse is not mere expression for expression's sake, but, as in the Aristotelian sense, in the service of the public good. It is about values, policies, and national character. Thus, Collins and Skover distinguish between the principles of political discourse characterized by rational decision-making, civic participation, meaningful dissent, and self-realization and contemporary political "speech" characterized by entertainment, passivity, pleasure, and self-gratification. They speculate that we are on the border of equating "amusement with enlightenment, fantasy with fact, and the base with the elevated."[28]

One should note that the concern is not about *oratory*, genuine engagement of ideas. As Keith Felton argues, "there is power in purposive oratory. When poetic in its reach, when deservedly acclaimed, oratory outlives the moment of utterance, and enters a universal lexicon of expression to become a permanently recorded part of the march of ideas. The influence of language upon history is ineluctable. . . . [It] buoys civilization over its perennial perils."[29]

MORAL LEADERSHIP

In my opinion, there exists a lack of moral leadership in all sectors of human society. Perhaps the most outspoken elected official lamenting the decline of American morals and character, Arkansas governor Mike Huckabee, argues, "Over the past thirty years, a decline in moral character has produced a decline in the character of our society."[30] The lack of moral leadership is demonstrated in the continuous uncovering of unethical behavior at all levels of society, from denials of risks to public safety from corporations to illicit acts in the halls within the White House. If indeed the American public has no concern about the character of our leaders, then it is a clear reflection on the moral condition of us the citizens.

Certainly since the 1960s many of our moral traditions, social values, and institutions have been challenged and frankly weakened. The result is a state of moral confusion and social relativism. In redefining the role of church, family, and education in American life, a vacuum developed. Once schools transmitted moral and social values of previous generations. Churches provided guidelines of behavior and personal moral expectations. Yes, perhaps those traditional values were too authoritarian. But nothing new replaced the old. The young have not lost their compass as much as they were never given one.

We need to return to a society in which certain actions are viewed as wrong. We need to get to a place and time when some things are not disputed in terms of right and wrong. I am not suggesting that we return to the values of the fifties, but indeed that we acknowledge some set of social virtues, some set of basic values that we all affirm. As Marvin Olasky recognizes, "before Americans can succeed in placing a moral leader at the top, we must develop a consensus on the importance of integrity; once that is in place, the likelihood of finding a person who can perform all of the presidential functions is increased."[31]

I am well aware that I will be summarily criticized and even dismissed, especially by academic colleagues, for even using the word *moral*. It sounds preachy, self-righteous, or sanctimonious. Indeed, among academics, the first protest will be the simple question, "Yeah, but whose values?" My initial response is simply "our values." For as a nation, we do have and can identify moral values. The issue is one of judgment. Are we willing to render judgment about failed expectations and performance? Thus, I am personally less concerned about the set of values than the implementation of those values as essential part of public and communal life.

I would argue that today, as never before, we should *select* moral leaders. We should actively seek those who reflect the very best of personal values and integrity. As argued earlier, our expectations should exceed those of the private sector. The presidency, in the words of Franklin Roosevelt, "is preeminently a place of moral leadership."[32]

The president is and should be a role model. The office reflects the values, hopes, and aspirations of the nation. We cannot tolerate a double standard, where we allow leaders to say one thing and do another, or violations of our social norms of expected behavior. Leadership is more than words. Leaders must act and must do so only in the context of their beliefs and values. Without action or principles, no one can become a leader. Leadership and the most basic of all human ethics are inextricably woven together. The president of the United States is more than a manager. Presidents are leaders.

Presidents *need* to be heroes for the young Americans, the children and future leaders of our country. As Peggy Noonan observes, "the young are moved by greatness. They are inspired by it. Children need heroes. They need them to lift life, to suggest a future you can be hungry for. They need them because heroes, just by being, communicate the romantic and yet realistic idea that you can turn your life into something great. The key, of course, is to have the right heroes—to be lifted by greatness and not just by glamour, to be lit by the desire to do good, as opposed to the desire to do well."[33] And we need to return to the "heroic" presidency. Bruce Miroff admits that Ronald Reagan represented the resurrection of the heroic presidency, at least for most of his administration. For him, Reagan's presidency "was a triumph of spectacle as well as substance. It showed how a president could sustain a larger-than-life persona and be presented by his public-relations specialists as the embodiment of cherished American self-images."[34] However, in a more recent work, Miroff expresses the fear that our "postmodern mood" threatens the reassertion of morals and principles by political leaders. "A public schooled in postmodern skepticism by a distrustful press will look for the political payoff every time it hears professions of virtue. Perhaps only a dramatic economic or social issue that galvanizes the public and redraws the map of partisan cleavages will move the Americans beyond postmodern detachment and irony."[35]

I am willing to accept the charge of being naïve. I do realize that individuals may be good administrators but poor leaders. I also understand that some immoral people may be successful managers. However, moral leadership implies standards of judgment and integrity. Values are so intrinsic to our thoughts and behaviors that we are unaware of their influence upon us. Even worse, we seldom reflect upon our personal or societal values. But virtually all of our conduct and behavior reflects some set of values. Values, most certainly, enter into virtually every decision a president makes.[36]

Moral leadership is especially required in a democracy because of the unique relationship between the elected servant and the citizenry. There is a strong correlation between public trust and government and the moral authority or character of the presidency. "Moral authority comes from trust and with trust there can be great synergy. Do not underestimate the power and value of moral authority. It is essential; and it depends on trust."[37]

Citizen trust is a critical element of democratic life. Much of today's rise in public alienation is fed by incessant scandal, and our mistrust has created political habits and institutions that now continue to produce ever more mistrust and cynicism. We continue to lose good people in public service. Take away public trust in the president and, as James Barber succinctly predicted, "we the people may turn him into an entertainer, who, however seriously he may take himself, need not furrow our brows with real-world calculation. . . . Presidential campaigns become an extended political holiday—a trip to the nation's psychological beaches and mountains—a 'suspension of disbelief' analogous to the restful anticipation one feels just as the lights go down and the curtain goes up in the theatre. The distinction fades between actors who play candidates or Presidents (Robert Redford, Henry Fonda) and Presidents struggling to act winningly in an essentially playful politics."[38]

Of course, it would help to return to the citizen legislator, the public servant, and not to professional politicians who spend their careers acquiring power, becoming rather superficial, photogenic, and poll-driven. With citizen legislators and leaders, we would get authentic messages, not the rhetoric of saying what they think we want to hear, or even worse, saying and doing anything to simply get elected.

Charles Goodsell argues that effective governmental leadership is fostered by a concept of what he calls "political professionalism." The concept embodies a set of normative principles that include a competence for power, a capacity for synthesis, an ability to exercise discretion within constraints, and possession of a service ethos.[39] It is, of course, the "ability to exercise discretion within constraints" that is useful to our consideration. Goodsell argues that one of the characteristics of any profession is "a substantial degree of collective self-governance through standard setting and regulation of conduct by the profession itself."[40]

Perhaps the most important link between the selection of moral leadership is moral followership. It takes good people to elect good people. How can government be as good as the American people?

CONSTITUTIONAL AUTHORITY AND PUBLIC MORALITY

The notion of authority is a central concept in social and political thought. There are many forms of authority: bureaucratic, technical, or professional, to name a few. But all forms of authority are based upon the structure of the social relationship between an individual and the state. Such a relationship may range from coercion based upon force, to unreflecting obedience based upon habit, to enlightened deference based upon a sense of values. The role of authority in government is not only in upholding moral, ethical, and intellectual standards but also in guaranteeing social and political freedom, and acting as a barrier to centralized, arbitrary, and despotic power. We use authority to protect our rights, to provide order and security, to manage conflict, and to distribute the benefits and burdens of society.

The authority of our government, its very structure, rules, and laws, originates from the constitution. The *moral* authority of government originates from the collective beliefs, attitudes, and values of the citizens. Moral authority may be generally defined as the felt obligations and duties derived from shared community values, ideas, and ideals. From a democratic perspective, the very nature of authority, as defined as the ability to evoke purely voluntary compliance, must be moral in form and content. Otherwise, social violence, chaos, and coercion will be the norm. A social hierarchy is maintained by a willing acceptance of the social order, a unifying set of common values, and a worldview that enshrines and legitimizes the established order. Moral authority rests on voluntary consent. Thus, from my view, democracy cannot exist without values. And political values are the distillation of principles from a systematic order of public beliefs.

Today, in the new millennium, what would a survey of our social and political landscape reveal? As one who has studied and written about American politics and political campaigns for more than twenty years, I am alarmed, concerned, and even saddened by our political climate and the attitudes reflected in our society today. As already noted, there exists among the public a climate of change, a climate of distrust, and even a climate of fear in terms of the future. And on all levels of measurement,

Americans participate less and are less concerned about and interested in affairs of state, even in this era of post-9/11 and world terrorism, especially among the young adults.

In the aftermath of winning the Cold War, the political climate became one of public distrust and cynicism. As demonstrated in earlier chapters, according to public opinion polls, many Americans have lost confidence in their government and trust in elected officials and politicians. Government and the political process were viewed as dominated by special interest rather than notions of the "common good" for all Americans. Citizens felt caught between the crossfire of self-interested politicians, special-interest groups, and large corporations. In 1995, Francis Fukuyama wrote that Americans were experiencing a genuine "crisis of trust."

The primary characteristic of our society in the nineteenth and the early twentieth centuries is that of a social contract. We attempted to build a comfortable society based upon a covenant, contract, or agreement for the mutual advantage of the members of society, the citizens and the government. Essentially, free people govern by free agreement. The rise of contractual relationships results in the elimination of autocratic, repressive, and coercive governments and the replacement of them with governments contractually elected, limited in power, and contractually obligated to respect the rights and specified liberties of the citizens. By means of our Constitution, the Bill of Rights, and common laws, the very values and prerogatives of society are promulgated and virtually guaranteed: freedom of religion, speech, the press, and assembly, to name a few. Contractual government is democratic government, a "government of the people, by the people, and for the people."

Thus, at the heart of democracy is the notion of a contract. And at the heart of any contract is the notion of trust. There was a time in America when citizens understood the terms of the relationship or contract with government and with each other that was based upon trust. The concept is very simple. I won't kill you if you won't kill me. I'll help protect your property if you help protect mine. I'll help build your barn if you will help build mine. If something happens to me, I know that as members of the larger community, my children and family will be protected and taken care of. Our contract with each other was based on mutual respect, honesty, and responsibility.

Our contract with government was based on trust too. A government, as the immortal words portray, "of the people, by the people, and for the people." It meant that the common good would prevail. Government, in all its actions, would be fair and just, and would operate in the interests of all citizens. Today, it appears that we no longer trust government, corporations, or even each other. We are now divided, as some say a "50/50" nation, either of the "red" or "blue" states. For too many Americans, our social contract has become null and void. Ultimately we are all in a mental state of psychological egoism—all interest is self-interest.

A government is only as good, decent, and moral as its citizens. The conduct of civil affairs in America has always occurred under a cloud of considerable public distrust. This distrust is an important but largely negative backdrop that conveys meaning to every other part of the nation's life. James Madison, in the Federalist Papers, number 51, recognized the tension between the need for a centralized government and a free people. He wrote,

> The interest of the man must be connected with the constitutional rights of the place. It may be a reflection on human nature that such devices should be necessary to control the abuses of government. But what is government itself but the greatest of all reflections on human nature? If men were angels, no government would be necessary. If angels were to govern men, neither external nor internal controls on government would be necessary. In framing a government which is to be administered by men over men, the great difficulty lies in this: you must first enable the government to control the governed; and in the next place oblige it to control itself. A dependence on the people is, no doubt, the primary control on the government.

Individual integrity, responsibility, and accountability are the best check on government abuse. An individual's moral judgments are dependent upon the administration of moral dignity and action.

The collective social values of the citizens become the conditions necessary for the existence of political authority. The government that encompasses and expresses our collective values ensures the respect and voluntary compliance of all citizens. Political authority rests on the assumption that it exists to promote the good of those who accept it, that the common good will prevail, not the self-interests of those in authority or those who exercise force.

By its nature, politics encourages a wary skepticism. And the traditions borne out of the nation's emergence honor the idea of freedom as a protection against governmental power that can easily be abused. Even so, today there has been an intensification of public distrust in many basic American institutions. There seems to be an increasing disconnect between the nation and its civic life. Paradoxically, while we have never had more access to the processes and moments of the political process, we have never felt less a part of the process.

A GOVERNMENT AS GOOD AS THE PEOPLE

The challenge is clear. As a nation, our greatest threat is internal, not external. We must stem the growing tide toward political cynicism and despair. First, we must find common themes and values that transcend our ever-deepening cultural differences. The notorious "red states versus blue states" dichotomy may be exaggerated, but harmful nonetheless. We must all be able to identify, to articulate, and to appreciate the core values of America. We need to reaffirm ourselves to our national civic values—the principles embodied in the Declaration of Independence, the Constitution, and the Bill of Rights—that bring us together as a people. The ideals of freedom, equality, democracy, and justice provide the basis for building community and trust in America today. How can we survive as a society if we deny commonality and praise autonomous individual behavior? We need some common acceptance of what is acceptable, what is fundamentally right and wrong, good and bad.

Second, civic responsibility, accountability, and initiative should once again become a keystone of social life. Moral discipline means using social norms, rules, customs, and laws to develop moral reasoning, self-control, and a generalized respect for others. Such an approach to social life will help citizens recognize the values behind the laws and why laws are needed, and will increase the feeling of moral obligation to respect government institutions. Democracy, as government "of the people, by the people, and for the people," shapes the form and content of political action in America. Democracy makes government accessible and accountable to ordinary citizens.

Finally, of course, we desperately need moral leadership in the future, not defined by a specific set of standards or dogma, but clearly recognized by the public as possessing the moral authority of governing. In short, in order to elect better leaders, we must become better citizens, friends, and neighbors. As Governor Huckabee declares, "Character is the issue, and your character makes a difference every day—in the work you do, the candidates you vote for, the people who look for you for leadership."[41] His call for action is straightforward. "There *is* something you can do about it: you can live a God-centered life of high moral character, and you can run for public office or support candidates who share your Christian standards. At first that sounds like an oversimplification—maybe even an impossibility—but I can tell you from personal experience that it can happen."[42] A genuinely moral nation will elect moral leaders.

We cannot change the very simple fact that we live in a world of increasing deception. We can't stop others from lying. But we can become truth seekers who are more discerning about whom to trust and how much. We can begin to recognize how people distort our reality and divert our search for truth. We need to quite simply pay *more* attention, not less, to the private decency, private morality, honesty, and honor of political candidates.

Bert Rockman concurs and opines that the central question for anyone studying leadership should be just what are the constraints imposed on and opportunities open to the specific leader. For him, to answer this question, one needs to focus on the individual leader and the repertoire of aptitudes and deficiencies for the presidential role.[43]

I readily acknowledge that no one leader can meet all the needs of the citizens in a democracy. I also acknowledge that no one leader can make or break our democracy. It would take a whole series of disastrous choices for us to undo the work of our forefathers. And I do believe that collectively, we the people are too smart to go down a path to jeopardize our nation.

However, leaders are important, especially in a democracy. They do more than initiate policy; they also symbolize the ideas and ideals of our nation. A healthy democracy will seek those who hold to certain moral requirements. We need leaders whose words are their bond, for democracy is a matter of faith in the collective wisdom of the citizens. If leaders say one thing and do another, how far can we trust them in any other sort of dealings?

I have the same fears and concerns about the state of our polity as I did nearly thirty years ago when I was immersed in my first presidential campaign. The campaign words of Jimmy Carter in 1975 ring true today.

It is time for us to reaffirm and to strengthen our ethical and spiritual and political beliefs. There must be no lowering of these standards, no acceptance of mediocrity in any aspect of our private or public lives. It is obvious that the best way for our leaders to restore their credibility is to be credible, and in order for us to be trusted we must be trustworthy! In our homes or at worship we are ever reminded of what we ought to do and what we ought to be. Our government can and must represent the best and the highest ideals of those of us who voluntarily submit to its authority. In our nation's third century, we must meet these simple but crucial standards.[44]

Perhaps we should not only ask the question, "Why not the best?" but demand nothing less from those who seek to serve.

NOTES

1. Clinton Rossiter, *The American Presidency*, Revised edition (New York: Mentor Books, 1962), 228.
2. Rossiter, *The American Presidency*, 237.
3. Daniel Boorstin, *The Image* (New York: Atheneum, 1962), 47–74.
4. Dan Nimmo and James Combs, *Mediated Political Realities*, 2nd edition (New York: Longman, 1990), 26.
5. Robert E. Denton, Jr., and Rachel L. Holloway, "Presidential Communication as Mediated Conversation: Interpersonal Talk as Presidential Discourse," in *Research in Political Sociology*, 7, 1995, 91–115.
6. Joe Klein, "The Bill Clinton Show," *Newsweek*, October 26, 1992, 35.
7. Roderick Hart, *The Sound of Leadership* (Chicago: University of Chicago Press, 1987), 54.
8. Joseph Straubhaar and Robert LaRose, *Media Now: Communications Media in the Information Age* (Belmont, CA: Wadsworth, 2000), 1–6.
9. Kathleen H. Jamieson, *Eloquence in an Electronic Age* (New York: Oxford University Press, 1988).
10. Denton and Holloway, "Presidential Communication as Mediated Conversation," 91–115.
11. Sanford Schram, "The Post-Modern Presidency and the Grammar of Electronic Engineering," *Critical Studies in Mass Communication*, 8, 1991, 210–16.
12. Franko Ferrarotti, *The End of Conversation* (Westport, CT: Greenwood, 1988), 13.
13. Roderick Hart, *Seducing America* (New York: Oxford University Press, 1994), 12.
14. Martin Schram, *The Great American Video Game* (New York: William Morrow, 1987), 215.
15. Joseph N. Cappella and Kathleen Hall Jamieson, *Spiral of Cynicism: The Press and the Public Good* (New York: Oxford University Press, 1997), 22.
16. Cappella and Jamieson, *Spiral of Cynicism*, 31.
17. Jamieson, *Eloquence in an Electronic Age*, 215.
18. Straubhaar and LaRose, *Media Now*, 428–29.
19. Peter Dahlgren, *Television and the Public Sphere* (Thousand Oaks, CA: Sage, 1995), 8.
20. Bruce Gronbeck, "The Ethical Performances of Candidates," in *Political Communication Ethics: An Oxymoron?* Robert E. Denton, Jr., ed. (Westport, CT: Praeger, 2000), 1–21.
21. Jurgen Habermas, *The Structural Transformation of the Public Sphere* (Cambridge, UK: Polity Press, 1989). (Original work published in German in 1962.)
22. Dahlgren, *Television and the Public Sphere*, 8.
23. Samuel Kernell, *Going Public* (Washington, DC: Congressional Quarterly Press, 1993).

24. Mary Stuckey and Frederick Antczak, "The Rhetorical Presidency: Deepening Vision, Widening Exchange," in *Communication Yearbook 21*, Michael Roloff and Gaylen Paulson, eds. (Thousand Oaks, CA: Sage, 1998), 422.

25. George Edwards, "Building Coalitions," *Presidential Studies Quarterly*, 30, 2000, 47–61.

26. William Lewis, "Telling America's Story: Narrative Form and the Reagan Presidency," *Quarterly Journal of Speech*, 78, 1987, 280–302.

27. Ronald Collins and David Skover, *The Death of Discourse* (Boulder, CO: Westview, 1996), xix.

28. Collins and Skover, *The Death of Discourse*, 203.

29. Keith S. Felton, *Warrior's Words: A Consideration of Language and Leadership* (Westport, CT: Praeger, 1995), xv.

30. Mike Huckabee, *Character Is the Issue* (Nashville, TN: Broadman & Holman, 1997), 1.

31. Marvin Olasky, *The American Leadership Tradition* (New York: Free Press, 1999), 270.

32. As quoted in Michael Genovese, *The Presidential Dilemma* (New York: HarperCollins, 1995), 151.

33. Peggy Noonan, "Three Presidents, One Lesson," *Wall Street Journal*, editorial page, February 9, 2001.

34. Bruce Miroff, "From 'Midcentury' to Fin-de-Siecle: The Exhaustion of the Presidential Image," *Rhetoric & Public Affairs*, 1 (2), 1998, 191.

35. Bruce Miroff, "Courting the Public," in *The Postmodern Presidency*, Steven Schier, ed. (Pittsburgh: University of Pittsburgh Press, 2000), 122.

36. William Hitt, *Ethics and Leadership* (Columbus, OH: Battelle Press, 1990), 5–6.

37. Len Marrella, *In Search of Ethics* (Sanford, FL: DC Press, 2001), 182.

38. James David Barber, *The Presidential Character* (Englewood Cliffs, NJ: Prentice Hall, 1972).

39. Charles Goodsell, "Political Professionalism," in *Executive Leadership*, Robert Denhardt and William Stewart, eds. (Tuscaloosa: University of Alabama Press, 1992), 7.

40. Goodsell, "Political Professionalism," 16.

41. Huckabee, *Character Is the Issue*, 3.

42. Huckabee, *Character Is the Issue*, 2.

43. Bert Rockman, "Cutting *With* the Grain: Is There a Clinton Leadership Legacy?" in *The Clinton Legacy*, Colin Campbell and Bert Rockman, eds. (New York: Chatham House, 2000), 276.

44. Jimmy Carter, *Why Not the Best?* (Nashville, TN: Broadman, 1975), 154.

Selected Bibliography

Ambrose, Stephen. "Dwight D. Eisenhower," in *Character Above All*, Robert A. Wilson, ed. New York: Simon & Schuster, 1995.

Aristotle. *Nicomachean Ethics*. W. D. Ross, J. L. Ackrill, J. O. Urmson, and D. Ross, translators. New York: Oxford University Press, 1998.

Barber, James. *The Presidential Character*. Englewood Cliffs, NJ: Prentice Hall, 1972.

Bennett, William. *The Death of Outrage*. New York: Free Press, 1998.

Blaney, Joseph, and William Benoit. *The Clinton Scandals and the Politics of Image Restoration*. Westport, CT: Praeger, 2001.

Boorstin, Daniel. *The Image*. New York: Atheneum, 1962.

Bovard, James. *"Feeling Your Pain."* New York: St. Martin's Press, 2000.

Buchanan, Bruce. *The Citizen's Presidency*. Washington, DC: Congressional Quarterly, 1987.

Buchanan, Bruce. *The Presidential Experience*. Englewood Cliffs, NJ: Prentice Hall, 1978.

Burns, James McGregor. *The Power to Lead*. New York: Simon & Schuster, 1984.

Campbell, Colin, and Bert Rockman, eds. *The Clinton Legacy*. New York: Chatham House, 2000.

Cannon, Carl. "Bush and God." *National Journal*, January 3, 2004, 12–17.

Cannon, James. "Gerald R. Ford," in *Character Above All*, Robert A. Wilson, ed. New York: Simon & Schuster, 1995.

Cappella, Joseph N., and Kathleen Hall Jamieson. *Spiral of Cynicism: The Press and the Public Good*. New York: Oxford University Press, 1997.

Carter, Jimmy. *Why Not the Best?* New York: Bantam, 1975.

Carter, Stephen. *Integrity*. New York: HarperCollins, 1996.

Ceasar, James, and Andrew Busch. *The Perfect Tie*. Lanham, MD: Rowman & Littlefield, 2001.

Collins, Ronald, and David Skover. *The Death of Discourse*. Boulder, CO: Westview, 1996.

Corwin, Edward. *The President: Office and Powers*, 3rd ed. New York: New York University Press, 1948.

Coulter, Ann. *High Crimes and Misdemeanors*. Washington, DC: Regnery, 1998.

Cronin, Thomas. *The State of the Presidency*. Boston: Little, Brown, 1975.

Dahlgren, Peter. *Television and the Public Sphere*. Thousand Oaks, CA: Sage, 1995.

Denton, Robert E., Jr., ed. *Political Communication Ethics: An Oxymoron?* Westport, CT: Praeger, 2000.

Denton, Robert E., Jr., ed. *The 2000 Presidential Campaign: A Communication Perspective*. Westport, CT: Praeger, 2002.

Denton, Robert E., Jr., and Rachel L. Holloway. "Presidential Communication as Mediated Conversation: Interpersonal Talk as Presidential Discourse." *Research in Political Sociology* 7 (1995): 91–115.

Drew, Elizabeth. *On the Edge*. New York: Simon & Schuster, 1994.

Edelman, Murray. *The Symbolic Uses of Politics*. Urbana: University of Illinois Press, 1964.

Edelman, Murray. *Politics as Symbolic Action*. Chicago: Markham, 1971.

Edelman, Murray. "The Politics of Persuasion," in *Choosing the President*, James D. Barber, ed. Englewood Cliffs, NJ: Prentice Hall, 1974.

Felton, Keith. *Warrior's Words: A Consideration of Language and Leadership*. Westport, CT: Praeger, 1995.

Ferrarotti, Franko. *The End of Conversation*. Westport, CT: Greenwood, 1988.

Fisher, Walter. "Rhetorical Fiction and the Presidency." *Quarterly Journal of Speech* 66, no. 2 (April 1980): 119–26.

Garment, Suzanne. *Scandal: The Culture of Mistrust in American Politics*. New York: Anchor Books, 1991.

Genovese, Michael. *The Presidential Dilemma*. New York: HarperCollins, 1995.

Greenberg, Paul. *No Surprises*. Washington, DC: Brassey's, 1996.

Greenstein, Fred, ed. *The George W. Bush Presidency: An Early Assessment*. Baltimore: Johns Hopkins University Press, 2003.

Gregg, Gary, and Mark Rozell, eds. *Considering the Bush Presidency*. New York: Oxford University Press, 2004.

Habermas, Jurgen. *The Structural Transformation of the Public Sphere*. Cambridge, UK: Polity Press, 1989. (Original work published in German in 1962.)

Hall, Peter. "A Symbolic Interactionist Analysis of Politics." *Sociological Inquiry* 42, nos. 3–4 (1972): 35–73.

Hart, Roderick. *The Sound of Leadership*. Chicago: University of Chicago Press, 1987.

Hart, Roderick. *Seducing America*. New York: Oxford University Press, 1994.

Heith, Diane. "Polling for a Defense: The White House Public Opinion Apparatus and the Clinton Impeachment." *Presidential Studies Quarterly* 30, no. 4 (2000): 783–90.

Hitchens, Christopher. *No One Left to Lie To.* New York: Verso, 1999.

Hitt, William. *Ethics and Leadership.* Columbus, OH: Battelle Press, 1990.

Huckabee, Mike. *Character Is the Issue.* Nashville, TN: Broadman & Holman, 1997.

Hughes, Emmet. *The Living Presidency.* New York: Penguin, 1974.

Jamieson, Kathleen H. *Eloquence in an Electronic Age.* New York: Oxford University Press, 1988.

Jones, Charles. *The Trusteeship Presidency.* Baton Rouge: Louisiana State University Press, 1988.

Kanungo, Rabindra, and Manuel Mendonca. *Ethical Dimensions of Leadership.* Thousand Oaks, CA: Sage, 1996.

Kellerman, Barbara. *Reinventing Leadership.* Albany: State University of New York Press, 1999.

Kernell, Samuel. *Going Public.* Washington, DC: Congressional Quarterly Press, 1993.

Kessler, Ronald. *A Matter of Character.* New York: Sentinel, 2004.

Klein, Joe. *The Natural.* New York: Doubleday, 2002.

Kouzes, James, and Barry Posner. *Leadership Challenge,* 3rd ed. San Francisco: Jossey-Bass, 2002.

Kulter, Stanley. *The Wars of Watergate.* New York: Alfred A. Knopf, 1990.

Kurtz, Howard. *Spin Cycle: Inside the Clinton Propaganda Machine.* New York: Free Press, 1998.

Lewis, William. "Telling America's Story: Narrative Form and the Reagan Presidency." *Quarterly Journal of Speech* 78 (1987): 280–302.

Lowry, Rich. *Legacy: Paying the Price for the Clinton Years.* Washington, DC: Regnery, 2003.

Marrella, Len. *In Search of Ethics.* Sanford, FL: DC Press, 2001.

McCullough, David. "Harry S. Truman," in *Character Above All,* Robert A. Wilson, ed. New York: Simon & Schuster, 1995.

Miroff, Bruce. "The Contemporary Presidency: Moral Character in the White House: From Republican to Democratic." *Presidential Studies Quarterly* 29 (Fall 1999): 708–12.

Miroff, Bruce. "Courting the Public," in *The Postmodern Presidency: Bill Clinton's Legacy in U.S. Politics,* Steven Schier, ed. Pittsburgh: University of Pittsburgh Press, 2000.

Nelson, Michael, ed. *The Election of 2000.* Washington, DC: Congressional Quarterly Press, 2001.

Nimmo, Dan. *Political Communication and Public Opinion in America.* Santa Monica, CA: Goodyear, 1978.

Nimmo, Dan, and James Combs. *Mediated Political Realities,* 2nd ed. New York: Longman, 1990.

Noonan, Peggy. "Ronald Reagan," in *Character Above All,* Robert A. Wilson, ed. New York: Simon & Schuster, 1995.

Novak, Michael. *Choosing Our King.* New York: Macmillan, 1974.

Olasky, Marvin. *The American Leadership Tradition*. New York: Free Press, 1999.

Olson, Barbara. *The Final Days*. Washington, DC: Regnery, 2001.

Parry-Giles, Shawn J., and Trevor Parry-Giles, *Constructing Clinton*. New York: Peter Lang, 2002.

Patterson, Robert. *Dereliction of Duty*. Washington, DC: Regnery, 2003.

Pious, Richard. "The Paradox of Clinton Winning and the Presidency Losing." *Political Science Quarterly* 114, no. 4 (Winter 1999): 569–93.

Podhoretz, John. *Bush Country*. New York: St. Martin's Press, 2004.

Pomper, Gerald, ed. *The Election of 2000*. New York: Chatham House, 2001.

Putnam, Robert. *Making Democracy Work: Civic Traditions in Modern Italy*. Princeton, NJ: Princeton University Press, 1993.

Raichur, Arvind, and Richard Waterman, "The Presidency, the Public, and the Expectations Gap," in *The Presidency Reconsidered*, Richard Waterman, ed. Itasca, IL: F. E. Peacock, 1993.

Reeves, Richard. *Running in Place*. Kansas City, KS: Andrews and McMeel, 1966.

Regan, Richard. *The Moral Dimensions of Politics*. New York: Oxford University Press, 1986.

Renshon, Stanley A., ed. *The Clinton Presidency*. Boulder, CO: Westview, 1995.

Renshon, Stanley A. *High Hopes: The Clinton Presidency and the Politics of Ambition*. New York: New York University Press, 1996.

Rossiter, Clinton. *The American Presidency*, Revised edition. New York: Mentor Books, 1962.

Rozell, Mark, and Clyde Wilcox, eds. *The Clinton Scandal and the Future of American Government*. Washington, DC: Georgetown University Press, 2000.

Schier, Steven, ed. *The Postmodern Presidency*. Pittsburgh: University of Pittsburgh Press, 2000.

Schippers, David. *Sellout*. Washington, DC: Regnery, 2000.

Schmidt, Susan, and Michael Weisskopf. *Truth at Any Cost*. New York: HarperCollins, 2001.

Schram, Martin. *The Great American Video Game*. New York: William Morrow, 1987.

Schram, Sanford. "The Post-Modern Presidency and the Grammar of Electronic Engineering." *Critical Studies in Mass Communication* 8 (1991): 210–16.

Shogan, Robert. *The Double-Edged Sword*. Boulder, CO: Westview, 2000.

Shogan, Robert. *Bad News: Where the Press Goes Wrong in the Making of the President*. Chicago: Ivan R. Dee, 2001.

Spitzer, Robert. "The Presidency: The Clinton Crisis and Its Consequences," in *The Clinton Scandal and the Future of American Government*, Mark Rozell and Clyde Wilcox, eds. Washington, DC: Georgetown University Press, 2000.

Stephanopoulos, George. *All Too Human.* Boston: Little, Brown, 1999.

Straubhaar, Joseph, and Robert LaRose. *Media Now: Communications Media in the Information Age.* Belmont, CA: Wadsworth, 2000.

Stuckey, Mary, and Frederick Antczak. "The Rhetorical Presidency: Deepening Vision, Widening Exchange," in *Communication Yearbook* 21, Michael Roloff and Gaylen Paulson, eds. Thousand Oaks, CA: Sage, 1998.

Thompson, Carolyn, and James Ware. *The Leadership Genius of George W. Bush.* Hoboken, NJ: John Wiley & Sons, 2003.

Thompson, Dennis. *Political Ethics and Public Office.* Cambridge, MA: Harvard University Press, 1987.

Walden, Gregory. *On Best Behavior: The Clinton Administration and Ethics in Government.* Indianapolis, IN: Hudson Institute, 1996.

Waterman, Richard, Robert Wright, and Gilbert Clair. *The Image-Is-Everything Presidency.* Boulder, CO: Westview, 1999.

White, Theodore. *Breach of Faith.* New York: Atheneum, 1975.

Wiebe, Robert. *The Opening of American Society.* New York: Vintage, 1984.

Wildavsky, Aaron. *The Beleaguered Presidency.* New Brunswick, NJ: Transaction, 1991.

Index

Kamungo, Rabindra, 49
Kellerman, Barbara, 11, 53
Kendall, David, 72
Kennedy, John F., 8, 9, 23, 25, 33,
    46, 73, 98
Kennedy, Ted, 42, 100
Kernell, Samuel, 125
Kerry, John, 104, 105, 106, 108,
    112; presidential election
    campaign 2004, 102–9
Kessler, Ronald, 97
Khrushchev, Nikita, 4
Kilpatrick, James, 78
Klein, Joe, 25, 37, 69, 83, 99, 101,
    121
Kohut, Andrew, 109
Kouzes, James, 46, 48, 49, 51
Krov, Matthew, 81
Kumar, Martha, 62
Kurtz, Howard, 69

Lamberth, Royce, 65
Land, Richard, 100
LaRose, Robert, 123
Lawson, Guy, 100
leadership, 11; authentic, x;
    characteristics of most admired
    leaders, 49–50; content of, 46;
    context of, 46; effective political,
    129–30; five exemplary practices
    of, 46; historical presidential
    perspectives of, 47–48; moral
    leadership, xi, 2, 45–57, 49
    127–30; presidential, 10–13,
    22–24, 48–53; private versus
    public behavior, 50–51, 73–76,
    134; relationships and, 49–50;
    symbolic, 39–40; transforming, 56;
    trust and, 50–52; values and, 38
Lewinski, Monica, 3, 5, 17, 19, 45,
    63, 64, 65, 67, 70, 72, 73
Lewis, William, 126
liberalism, x

Lincoln, Abraham, 7, 40, 110
Locke, John, 50
Lowry, Rich, 65, 66, 67
lying, 3–5; Clinton and, 62–66;
    public, 4–5; trust and, 65; youth
    and, 3–4
Lynn, Barry, 101, 103

MacArthur, Douglas, 8
Madison, James, 47, 132
Marrella, Len, 54
McCullough, David, 54
McDougal, Susan, 79
McGovern, George, 42
McGregor, James, 56
McKinney, Gene, 75
McLaughlin, John, 79
Meacham, Jon, 107
Mendonca, Manuel, 49
Meyerson, Harold, 99
Miroff, Bruce, 23, 45, 46, 60, 66,
    70, 83, 128
moral authority: government and,
    130
moral capital, 49
moral leadership, xi, 2, 127–30;
    democracy and, 129; presidency
    and, 45–57
moral values, x, 2, 3, 127–28;
    presidential election campaign
    2004 and, 102–9
morality, 130–32
moral virtues, 48–49
Morris, Dick, 70, 72

Nader, Ralph, 101
national character, 3–7
Newcombe, John, 90
Nimmo, Dan, 38
Nixon, Richard, 5, 6, 12, 15, 17, 19,
    21, 25, 42, 46, 56, 59, 75, 77,
    78, 83, 94, 97, 110; character of,
    9, 10; Clinton comparison and,

77–78; "imperial" presidency of, 12; resignation of, 61; Watergate and, 9, 11, 19, 20, 23, 59–60, 77, 78
Noonan, Peggy, 55
Novak, Michael, 42

Olasky, Marvin, 51, 61, 78, 127
Olson, Barbara, 17, 80
O'Reilly, Bill, 101

Parry-Giles, Shawn, 24, 25, 60, 77
Parry-Giles, Trevor, 24, 25, 60, 77
Passion of the Christ, The (Gibson), 103
Patterson, Robert, 65, 75, 76
Perkins, Tony, 105
Perot, Ross, 42
Pious, Richard, 72
Plato, 3, 50
Podhoretz, John, 96, 99
political climate, 130–31
politicians: citizens and, 6; skepticism of, 6
politics: skepticism and, 6
Posner, Barry, 46, 48, 49, 51
postmodernism, 128
postmodern presidency, 24–26
Powers, Gary Francis, 4
presidency: approval ratings and, 18; behavior expectations of, 33; challenges for institution, 123–27; character and, 1–13, 7–10, 47–48, 53–56; character traits of, 47–48; constitutional job description of, 30–32; desired qualities of, 33–34; as diminished, 15–27; discourse and, 123, 125–27; ethics and, 4; expectations of, 32–35; failed leadership and, 22–23; as heroes, 128; heroic, x, 1, 60, 128; high public support of, 52; historical perspectives of leadership, 47–48;

institutional, 10–13; leadership and, 10–13, 22–24, 48–53; lying and, 4; managerial view of, 120–21; moral authority and, 75; moral leadership and, 45–57, 127–30; as paradox, 25; paradoxical nature of, 35–37; post-Clinton implications, 81–82; postmodernism and, 24–26; powers of, 31; public communication and, 121–23; public expectations of, 11; public's relationship with, 52–53; as role model, 1, 128; roles of, 31–32; as symbol, 38–43; symbolic nature of, 25–26, 38–43; trust and, 50–52
presidential election campaign 1992, 62, 63, 65
presidential election campaign 1996, 21
presidential election campaign 2000, x, 2, 6, 18, 20, 21, 89–94; moral values and, 102–9
presidential election campaign 2004, 99–100, 102–9
presidential leadership, 10–13, 22–24, 48–53
presidential lying, 4; Clinton and, 62–66
Price, Lucille, 97
private versus public behavior, 50–51, 73–76, 134
public: cynicism, 21, 23, 74; morality, 130–32
Putnam, Robert, 49

Raichur, Arvind, 18
Ralston, Joseph, 75
Rather, Dan, 104
Reagan, Ron, 101
Reagan, Ronald, 10, 18, 52, 81, 83, 101, 108, 128; "heroic presidency" and, 12

About the Author

Robert E. Denton, Jr., holds the W. Thomas Rice Chair of Leadership Studies and serves as director of the Major General W. Thomas Rice Center for Leader Development. He teaches in the Department of Communication at Virginia Polytechnic Institute and State University (Virginia Tech). Denton teaches courses in political communication, political campaigns, media and politics, and the American presidency. He has degrees in political science and communication from Wake Forest University and Purdue University. He served as host of a weekly half-hour television talk show for eleven years and works with various media outlets as political analyst and commentator. In addition to numerous articles, essays, and book chapters, Denton is author, coauthor, or editor of sixteen books. The most recent titles include *Language, Symbols, and the Media: Communication in the Aftermath of the World Trade Center Attack* and *The 2004 Presidential Campaign: A Communication Perspective*. Denton serves as editor for Rowman & Littlefield's series Communication, Media, and Politics.